How to Cure Depression and Anxiety

How to Cure Depression and Anxiety

C Viljoen

PARTRIDGE

To order additional copies of this book, contact
Toll Free 0800 990 914 (South Africa)
+44 20 3014 3997 (outside South Africa)
orders.africa@partridgepublishing.com

www.partridgepublishing.com/africa

Contents

Terms, Conditions & Disclaimer

Christoffel Jakobus Viljoen is the author, and copyright owner of the book "How to Cure Depression & Anxiety" and all of its content © 2012. All rights reserved. ®™ All information provided in this book is for educational and informational purposes only. This information should not replace proper evaluation and diagnosis of depression or anxiety or other medical conditions by a licensed medical and mental health professional. Before taking any action, please consult with a licensed medical and mental health professional. You receive this book and all of its content as is, without any representation as to its fitness for any purpose. In addition, you do not receive warranty of any kind, either expressed or implied, including without limitation the implied warranties and fitness for any particular purpose in its content. You do not receive any guarantee with respect to accuracy, completeness, errors, or omissions, of any content in this book. The author of this book and any of his representatives are under no obligation to provide support, updates, enhancements, or other modifications. In no event will the author of this book or any of his representatives be liable for any action taken, or any negative or costly outcome in reliance upon the information provided through this book. The author of this book, including all its content, and all the representatives of these entities, shall not be liable for any compensatory or non-compensatory damages, including but not limited to special, indirect, incidental, or consequential damages or loss of any kind, with respect to any claim arising out of or in connection with the use of this book, even if it has been or is hereafter advised of the possibility of such damages. By reading this book, you agree to be bound in all the terms and conditions stated in the "Terms, Conditions, & Disclaimer" section of this book.

Introduction

My name is Chris Viljoen, and I wrote this book to help those who suffer from depression effectively, and those who want to help loved-ones with depression. In this book, we also take a deep look at anxiety-related depression. It is important that you do everything you can do to feel better, even if you do not feel like it right now, but it is most important that you understand it better first!

Have you ever found yourself wondering why you are not like everybody else? Craving an answer to why you always feel so weak or tense, why your personality is not as fun as those of your friends, always asking yourself: "What is wrong with me?", "I'm always shy", "nobody likes me", "I'm worthless", "this stress is killing me", "I feel so weak, and tense, and tired, and sick"? Do you maybe know of someone who feels like this all the time? Well, then you should find this book very interesting and helpful.

This book talks about everything you might be wondering about, and though most examples in this book relate to major depression, it lists and discusses all common forms of depression and anxiety, along with their symptoms and solutions.

Here are some of the fundamental questions this book will answer:

1. What EXACTLY is depression and anxiety?
2. Why does it happen?
3. Where does it all start and where can it lead?
4. When will it end in "happily ever after"?
5. How do we get depressed, and how can we solve it?

6. Lastly, you will see a summary of everything covered and read a little motivation.

Something to note before we start:

- If you are going through some tough times, it is easy to misdiagnose yourself, and believe you have depression, while you actually suffer from something different. If you have a feeling that you might be suffering from depression, you should take it seriously and see a qualified professional, like a psychiatrist who can put you through a simple fifteen-minute test to determine if you do in fact have depression, and what you can do about it. Sadness and depression are two very different things!
- To find out more, or to contact the author, visit: www.chrisviljoen.org

Ok, let us start talking about this very important topic...

Chapter 1.1

The brain's neurology

So firstly, we will answer the question: "What EXACTLY is depression?"

There is a very easy way of knowing what depression really is! Do you feel tired, or not in the mood to do anything? Are you sad, or do you feel helpless, and hopeless, or unimportant? Do you consider yourself not worth loving? Do you struggle to fall asleep at night because of many racing thoughts? Are you saying yes to more than two of these examples? Maybe you are tense and stressed every day of your life? Well, then you might be suffering from depression or anxiety, but luckily this is only half the story.

What if you were told there are chemicals in your bloodstream that forces your brain to make you think and feel like this? Well, there are, and that means if you can fix these chemicals, and get more of the right ones flowing in your brain, you will feel much better! There are many causes for the way we feel sometimes, so we will discuss the chemical, as well as the psychological side! Let us start by having a look at how the brain works, and check out some chemicals that influence our feelings:

Billions of neurons and synapses exist in our brain that looks like tiny hairs, pointing toward each other. These words might sound intimidating, but you will understand them quite well as you read on.

Imagine plucking two hairs from your head and pointing them toward each other on a piece of white paper, leaving a very small opening between those two hairs. Your brain has billions of little hair-like structures just like this, going all over the place! Those hairs represent neurons in your brain, and they act like a road where information travels on. So remember, neurons are

1

information highways. The synapse is the little open space between the tips of these two hairs, and this is where information can move from one road, to another. Think about these synapses as ramps on the neuron-highway.

The information you think about moves through these neuron-roads, and it uses the synapses or "ramps" to get from one neuron-hair to another. Now you might be wondering how information can travel safely across those openings between two roads. Well, a chemical called "serotonin" exists in the tips of each of these neuron-hairs. This "serotonin" chemical is the main thing concerning depression and anxiety! Serotonin is the chemical that regulates your mood, and helps information to stay safe in your mind! There are a few other chemicals also, like GABA, but serotonin is "the" one! You will learn about serotonin shortly. Remember for now that there are billions of roads connected to each other in our brain.

With every one of our thoughts, our brain shoots electronic pulses from one neuron to another, sending information around our brain. You see, our brain has many different parts, like memory and processing. Think about this: If you want to tell someone about the 09/11 incident, information needs to travel from your memory and into a processor in your brain before you can tell someone about it! Does that make sense to you? Now when you want to think about something, here is exactly what will happen: An electronic pulse (or static pulse) will fire, sending the information from your memory to the tip of the first neuron-road. Here the information can climb into little "busses" of serotonin. This serotonin-chemical will capture the information, and then safely move the information out of the first neuron, through the synapse-ramp, and into the tip of the second neuron. After the serotonin empties out the information into the second neuron-hair, the serotonin can safely move back through the synapse into the first neuron and wait for you to think about something else. The information that is now in the tip of the second neuron moves further with another static pulse, where it will move into a processor, so you can "see" the things you are thinking about in your mind.

Bear with these names; you have only one more to learn! You are doing great so far! Neurotransmitters have the job of taking information into different neuron-hairs around our brain, and serotonin is one example of these neurotransmitter-chemicals. So first, we have an electronic signal, then a chemical signal, and then another electronic signal with every thought in our minds, but if the chemical signal is weak, the second electronic signal will also be weak, causing depression.

Are you still following? Serotonin enables us to think, but it also regulates our mood by telling our body when to create the other chemicals we need to have feelings.

Here is a more practical example:

Let us say you recently went on vacation and you saw the most beautiful sunset ever... After you get back, you still remember how it looks, and a week later, you want to tell someone about it. What will happen in your brain? Well, the image of the sunset will come out of your long-term memory banks, and move through a neuron until it reaches the tip. When the image of the sunset reaches the end of the first neuron-road, it will climb into a series of busses called serotonin. These little Serotonin busses will then transport the information through the synapse-ramp, and into the second hair. After the sunset image gets out of the busses, the empty serotonin busses will move back to their original first neuron-hair, and wait for more information. The information about the sunset that is now in the second hair will continue to move with electronic pulses on the second neuron-road, into a processor, so that you can see the image in your head and describe it to someone.

However, what if there is not enough of this Serotonin-chemical in your brain? Well, this is actually the cause of depression and anxiety, as you learnt earlier. Why, you may ask? Well, because serotonin also has the job of telling your body when to make other chemicals.

If there is not enough of this serotonin-chemical in your brain, many things will go wrong.

Here are some practical examples:

1. Your thinking becomes very slow, because every time information travels across your brain, this small amount of serotonin-busses need to make many more than just one trip to get the information out of one hair, into the second.

   In addition, you need to recall the same information many more times than once, because some serotonin that moves through the synapse, does not make it through to the second hair, and so it dissolves, causing you to forget that information you were thinking about, or to have difficulty remembering specific details.

This is why you may sometimes find yourself running to the kitchen, and forget what you wanted to do there. You may also struggle to concentrate on what you are busy doing. Get your brain full of serotonin and you will be able to remember new information a lot better! You will learn methods to do this later in this book! If more serotonin does not seem to help, it is because of low GABA levels! GABA is a chemical that helps your body to use serotonin. Do not feel discouraged! From this point on, everything is much easier to understand, and you are going to learn some amazing things!

2. In some cases of depression or anxiety, you might experience poor eyesight and this is not because your eyes and ears became weaker. The reason is also too little serotonin! Think about this: If your eyes see something, but there is too little serotonin to send the full image from your eyes into your brain, little particles of the image you are looking at will get lost, making your eyesight fuzzy. The same applies to your ears, your tongue, and all your other senses.

3. Eventually your whole body and brain will become much slower, because if there is not enough serotonin in your brain, it will have to take much more than just one trip to transport information around your brain. This prevents you from using a fast-paced instrument; it may become difficult for you to engage in social gatherings or to think up new ideas!

4. It makes your reflexes slower, and this leads to poor driving skills or slower reaction time when you encounter obstacles on the road. Low serotonin levels even cause sleepless nights, and raging emotions!

5. Would you like to know how this serotonin chemical regulates our mood? Well, little glands exist right through our entire body that create different chemicals for us. These glands look like small volcanoes, and some of them are in the stomach, while others are in the throat, and some are in many other various places. Some of the chemicals these glands create will make us feel good, and others make us feel distressed, or sad. For instance, your adrenalin glands are on your kidneys. Other glands also exist that create melatonin, dopamine, and endorphins, which are all chemicals that change our mood. If you eat

something that you really enjoy, your serotonin chemical will tell your body to create more dopamine, so you feel attracted to what you are eating and dopamine will motivate you to eat more. Serotonin also regulates a multitude of other things that I will show you later. So now you can see that because of too little serotonin, your whole body's chemicals will be unbalanced.

Some other physical things you may experience if you have depression are:

1. Headaches, severe stress and dizziness at times,
2. Complete inability to concentrate on what you are busy doing,
3. Extremely fast light-headedness when using social drugs and alcohol,
4. Your short-term memory is affected causing you to forget new information like shopping lists, people's faces, and names, or even driving directions almost instantly. Do you ever find yourself focussing on what someone is saying, and then immediately afterward you may ask that person to repeat what he or she said because it went right by you?
5. You become uninterested in doing things you once enjoyed, because it even becomes an effort for your brain just to laugh, or to pick up your arm.
6. Depressed people are not lazy, but it feels like everybody thinks they are! Some depressed people even say they are lazy, because their whole body feels tired and worn out constantly, even while they are young.
7. You may also get irritated and short-tempered quickly with everyone and everything, because it is an indescribably difficult task for your brain to think on even the easiest of things. Like eating, or watching a movie, and if anyone or anything interrupts your brain's difficulty to concentrate, your sub-conscious mind will automatically try to chase away the culprit, causing your brain to go into a defensive mode protecting itself from more information, like someone eating with their mouth open, or someone asking you a question. Usually these things may have never bothered you! Therefore, you are never in the mood for anyone or anything.
8. Even if you go to bed early, you are always tired the next morning, because you toss-and-turn endlessly in bed.

9. You also lose your appetite to eat almost completely, or in some rare cases, you may begin to eat excessively.
10. In addition, it is very easy for a depressed person to get sick, and very difficult to recover from illness. This is because the unbalanced chemicals in your body are affecting your immune system. Remember, if one chemical falls over, it will cause a chain-reaction and this causes some depressed people to get worse and worse.
11. These were the most basic things that happen in a depressed person's body, and not all of them may occur in a single patient. We will discuss some more experiences later.

You have to remember, that feeling depressed is just your brain sending chemical messages to your body telling you something is wrong. Think about nausea... If you feel like vomiting, it might be that you swallowed something that is poisoned, and it might harm you if it stays there. Can you imagine if your stomach did not tell your brain when it has a problem? You would not want that, and we do not want our brain not to tell us if a chemical imbalance in our body is busy harming us, because that is exactly what depression is! It might cause you to be more negative in the process, but that is just because you did not know the connection of depression-symptoms.

Sometimes the cause of depression is certain events in our past, triggering our body to imbalance its chemicals, and sometimes our past locks us up, and our temporary sadness becomes depression.

In other cases, it is just a normal imbalance of chemicals without any event causing it. Did you know that certain medication could cause depression? Another amazing fact is that the symptoms of depression are almost the same as that of diabetes and obesity!

You will learn more about how to know the difference later! You can see that all these cases have a chemical imbalance, and this imbalance causes our body to poison us with the chemicals that tell us what is wrong. That is why some people get heart attacks at 34, because of stress caused by a hidden depression.

Did anyone ever tell you "stress kills"? Well, it literally can eventually, because while you are depressed, your body only creates harmful and toxic chemicals. You might have heard that you can "think" yourself cured out of a cold, or another physical sickness. Well, that is also true, because if you can stay positive in the time of your sickness, the "feel-good" chemicals your brain will make in the process will certainly help the cold-medicine to work a lot faster! "Feel-good" chemicals are healthy! You CAN actually "think" some vitamins into your body! You just have to think good until you feel good. Laughter really is the strongest medicine, because it causes blood pressure to lower, endorphins to be created faster, nerves to relax, blood-flow to increase, and toxic stress chemicals to leave your body, all helping your immune system to become stronger against all forms of illness!

Would you like to have a list of the good chemicals your body can create, and learn how to get them going in your body without seeing a doctor? How about a list of bad chemicals too, so you know how to avoid them? Well, you are going to get it later in this book! Read on soldier!

Chapter 1.2

Some amazing chemical works

Ok, so far we have been answering the question: "What EXACTLY is Depression?" and we have learned that we need serotonin to help us think and feel better, because it helps our body create good chemicals and it stops us from poisoning ourselves. It also helps us stay healthy, and think fast. Did you think happiness falls out of the sky for everyone? Think again!

You have to know that no emotions are bad! No emotions are bad. It is good sometimes to feel depressed, or sad, when bad things happen in our lives. If you never have a sad emotion, you will not survive. No one will! Emotions simply tell us a very true story of how we react to things in our life, and what we sometimes allow ourselves to go through. In other cases our emotions tells us if something is not developed properly in our bodies that we should find a way to heal so that we can handle stress in our lives better. Did you know everyone experiences depression at some point, and for our whole lives, and that it is actually healthy? Let me explain:

Every day we go through some stress, whether at work, or at home, in our studies, or between our families and friends... Everyone has some form of strain in his or her lives every day, and we cannot avoid it! All your daily thinking damages your brain, almost like a muscle that experiences millions of little tears when it exercises.

Once every now-and-then, maybe once a month, or once every three months, our brain then goes into a slower state or a "mini-depression", so that it can heal itself to be ready for handling stress again. Most of us do not even know it ever happens, but without these little "mini-depressions", it is impossible for us to be alive!

Now before we continue, just remember that our body has a series of volcanoes, containing different chemicals, and it simply injects us with the chemical our brain feels like. These volcanoes are the little glands found all over our body and serotonin regulates these other glands. Serotonin is also a chemical, and it too has a gland of its own.

Now you might be wondering: How does a person's brain work who is not depressed?

Well, a healthy person's brain will be far more up-and-awake at most, because such a person has more serotonin injected into his bloodstream by his chemical glands! This means his brain can concentrate a lot easier on the positive things of life, and concentrate its attention more on injecting his body with all the other "feel-good" chemicals it has!

Here are the most important examples:

- Adrenalin is a feel-good chemical that allows you to be awake when you need to be, and it enables people to react allot faster to obstacles on the road, and to think and react very fast and more efficient in everything they do each day. Adrenalin also helps us feel more confident in general. It is an amazing chemical helping stamina in a person, and it makes the gym a fun place! It even makes muscles more powerful!

    Adrenalin is the "fight-or-flight" chemical, enabling you to fight quickly or run away quickly depending on the situation you are in at any specific time. Whenever your sub-conscious mind thinks you are in a life-threatening situation, it will tell your adrenal glands to produce a high dose of adrenalin, which is also known as epinephrine, along with other hormones that raise your heart rate, breathing and blood pressure. This causes a high dose of oxygen-rich blood to move to your brain and muscles needed for "fight or flight" responses, and it causes a rapid release of glucose and fatty acids causing your energy. Your senses also become keener, your memory sharper, your pupils will dilate causing you to see better, and you become less sensitive to pain. Your body always creates adrenalin, but it fires huge amounts of adrenalin when you are in a dangerous situation.

That is why some people may become overweight because of stress! Your body secretes a lot of adrenalin when you stress, but if you do not use that adrenalin by doing something physical with your body; your body will reserve the adrenalin as fat along with some other stress-chemicals.

This will cause you to feel fatigued (or tired without reason). A person who is not depressed feels amazingly great, and ready for life! Obviously, everyone encounters tiredness and bad times, but this is how we should all generally feel.

- A happy person's brain will also inject a lot more endorphins into that person's blood, which enables them to feel very much in love when they like someone! People with a higher dose of endorphins in their bodies will laugh a lot more in general, and it makes your body a lot less vulnerable to pain.

Why do you think you have more pain than others do when you get hurt? It is because your serotonin level is low, causing your endorphin chemical to also go down! Endorphin-junkies are tigers in bed, and stallions at the dinner table! Do you get the drift?

- Another good chemical happy people have a lot of, is dopamine, which is the "reward" hormone, or the "lust" hormone. Dopamine motivates us to do just about anything. Whether it is having sex, eating, taking risks, achieving goals, or drinking water, they all increase dopamine and that turns on the reward centre in our minds, wanting to achieve the best of that task. This means if you eat something you really enjoy, your brain will immediately inject your blood with more dopamine, giving you the thought of wanting "more... more... more..." until you are satisfied.

Dopamine motivates you to orgasm when you are having sex, or masturbating. Incidentally, this is why so many young people feel guilty after masturbating. Dopamine stops immediately after orgasm, causing you to come back to earth at high speed. It is nothing to be ashamed of, and there is nothing wrong with it! It is healthy, and if you are a Christian, it is not even a sin. The sin is dirty thinking while you are masturbating, but masturbating is not a sin. I dare you to find the evidence for yourself... That is if you disagree of course! Practice telling yourself that you feel great a few minutes after masturbating and you really will feel great every time soon. Be proud of masturbating when it is appropriate, because it is healthy, and God's way of helping teenagers cope with raging hormones as they grow!

If your body does not produce enough dopamine when you enjoy something, like in a depressed person, you might find it difficult at times to get sexually aroused, or to stay aroused for the entire duration of sex. You will not be motivated to do anything, and you also lose your appetite for eating or for doing things, you used to enjoy.

- Ephedrine is another great chemical your brain can inject into your body, and this one, along with some others, is one that gives your body great power and energy during the day!
- Your body constantly needs acetylcholine to send messages from your nerves to your muscles, allowing you to have full control over your muscles, and it enables the brain to learn and remember things. People with Alzheimer's disease or Parkinson's disease may have a specific neurological condition, but it may also be due to not having enough acetylcholine in their bloodstream. People who do not excel in sport may also have a shortage of acetylcholine in their bodies, and it may all be because of too little serotonin being created by your body.
- Your brain gives you melatonin at night, just before your biological clock tells you it is sleep time, allowing your body to switch off at night and fall into a nice comforting deep sleep quickly.

This "biological clock" thing is actually very interesting, and serotonin is the chemical that regulates it! That means if you do not have enough serotonin in your body, your biological clock will stop, making your resting time a disaster.

What happens is a lot of serotonin exists in a healthy person during the day, helping that person to have feelings, to focus, to think, and be awake. At night, the challenging events of the day have passed, leaving your brain exhausted and then it creates less serotonin on purpose so you can switch off and go to bed and rest, to recharge and feel healthy again the next day. It gets used to a pattern, and this is what creates our biological clock.

For a depressed person, this is not the case though. When a healthy person is awake, adrenalin starts rushing, and serotonin production speeds up. This means their brain is in the "alpha" state. The alpha state is the up-and-awake state, the thinking quick and feeling fresh state. Then later, when the healthy person goes to bed, their brain goes into a much slower "beta" state, allowing their body and mind to switch off and fall asleep.

The problem in a depressed person's brain is they are in the beta state the whole time. Even during the day. Feeling tired, slowed down, not in the mood to do anything, tensed up and full of aches and pains the whole time, because of poisonous chemicals damaging their body and rearranging their habits. By tired I do not mean feeling too lazy to get out of bed, I am talking about constantly having so little energy that it feels like you can collapse at any time, even as you are getting out of bed.

This makes it easy for us to be negative, increasing poisonous chemicals even more. For a healthy person, being sad or tired is temporary, but being depressed sticks until we fix it. Some anxiety-related depression causes people to be so anxious that it is impossible to stay calm. Do you think it is easy to be negative if you feel like this every day?

Ok, now just remember that a healthy person's brain will be in the alpha state the whole day, up until they get into bed. Here the brain will switch into the slower beta state. Now, when a depressed person goes to bed, they are already in the sleeping beta state, even before reaching the bed. They have been awake in the beta state the whole day, every day. When it is bedtime for a depressed person, the brain cannot step down to any slower state where you can fall asleep. That is why you toss-and-turn endlessly and experience many racing thoughts at night. Your body cannot switch off. You had to force it to stay awake during the switched-off beta state.

The only time you can fall asleep quickly, and go into a deep sleep, feeling refreshed the next morning, is if you can get enough serotonin in your brain, and do some other tips and tricks later in this book.

This will allow your brain to recalibrate its biological clock so that it is in the alpha state during the day, AND when you go to bed. Then when your brain notices you went to bed and you want to sleep, your brain can step down from fast alpha into slow beta. The beta state will then put you into a light sleep, and all the other states of dreaming, and being fast asleep can follow. If you go to bed already in the light-sleeping beta state like a depressed person, your brain cannot step down further because there is no initial sleep-starting phase after the beta state.

All these things happen because of a little gland in your body that is not creating enough of the good serotonin chemical your brain needs. Now because of this, your brain is going to tell you something is not right. Like the pain caused by a broken leg... That pain tells you something is wrong, and now you can help your body fix it! If your brain notices it is not receiving enough serotonin, it will start to tell you: "Hey, you better stress and do something, because you have a problem with your chemical glands!" It does this by overdosing your body with chemicals like cortisol and valium. These chemicals are good for you and they fight stress, but if they become an overdose as it is in a depressed person, it will cause stress and depression to get worse.

Here is what these chemicals do specifically:

- Cortisol is a stress-fighting chemical. However, if you are depressed, your body creates too much cortisol, and this means the stress-fighting cortisol will start to GIVE you stress and anxiety, instead of fighting it. Remember that serotonin regulates all the other chemicals, and so basically, if your body has too little serotonin, your body will make your depression worse and worse until you exercise the gland that produces the serotonin in your body. This will cause your body to stop overdosing you on cortisol. It will allow your body to create just enough so that you feel relaxed after a stressful event has passed.
- Another chemical your body can inject into your bloodstream is valium, which calms your body from anxiety after having an anxiety attack, or some form of hyper-activity. Valium is a mild depressor and causes a hypnotic or sleep-like effect, and in some cases, it can even be used to sedate patients. Leaving anxiety-related depression unattended may cause your body to constantly create too much of this valium chemical. This will worsen depression, or anxiety, and can even induce rage, depression, excitement, epilepsy and seizures or cause Parkinson's disease if the person with anxiety does not begin overcoming the anxiety soon enough.

Both cortisol and valium are the stress and anxiety fighting chemicals our body needs, but it causes some depressed people to get worse and worse if they do not fix the problem, because these chemicals overdose their bodies.

Now because your brain is not feeling happy, it will start to give your body some nice sharp doses of these "sadness chemicals" so your body can notice your thinking is blue for some reason, and it is taking too long. This is ok, but if it continues for long periods at once, like in a depressed person, these chemicals will harm your body causing you to get grey hair, or noses and ears to grow quicker, or go bald sooner, get sick quicker, and it changes your allergies. It will also change the way your stomach digests food, sometimes you can become infertile, and just about every molecule in your body behaves differently. You become impotent soon, your bone-structure becomes weak and brittle, your muscles weaken along with your heart, causing you to get tired sooner than you should, and many other things go wrong. Depression will even physically cause you to feel pain much quicker and more intense than others.

Luckily, none of this has to be permanent! You can fix it all! These sadness chemicals are not bad, because it tells you of a problem, or it helps a happy person to mourn when we all need to, or to calm down after a stressful event.

As you have learned it also helps your brain stay strong, but if a depressed person does not do anything about it, these chemicals will poison their body. Remember in the beginning of the book I told you that this is the reason young people start to look a lot older, and get heart attacks soon. Stress really kills! It is not just a mental thing; it really can physically kill you! We CAN reach 92, and still be fit enough to run the 94.7 marathon!

If you can force yourself to stop stressing about your problems, and if you can force yourself to feel good for long enough, all these bad side-effects of depression will reverse itself, making you look and feel young and energetic again. Medication, therapy, and some other methods mentioned later can help you with this task.

Now remember, if you feel depressed for long, your body is strong in creating bad chemicals. The only way you can fight it is by forcing yourself to feel good somehow! This sounds challenging right? Later you will read the tips that make this task easy. You have to think less and stress less about your problems and issues, so that your heart feels glad and energised, and your mind clear. Yes, it is difficult, and sometimes impossible, but this is why you can get medication to boost you for a while, and a therapist to teach you the ways of thinking clear and becoming positive, and to teach you the methods of a healthier lifestyle!

After an amount of time between a few weeks, or in some cases after a year or two, the medicine and therapy can stop, and you will be the best person you can be!

Becoming positive will cause your body to become strong in creating good chemicals, and it will automatically become weak in creating bad chemicals, because those poison-glands will become weak like muscles that do not exercise. Soon they will become unable to create overdoses of sad feelings, but just enough, so you can still experience sadness when you have to.

So do you want to feel better, happier, and not afraid anymore? Would you like it if you could feel sad or tired when you have to, without experiencing the symptoms of a long-term depression? Do you want to feel great every day, and sleep tight at night having rest that nothing can disturb?

Do you want to see how wonderful and great you really are, even though you do not believe in it right now? Do you want to look and feel young, sexy, and excited about your life again, actually having the urge and confidence to go to the gym every day without quitting? Do you want unnecessary sadness to disappear?

Well you know what, throughout the book you will learn many ways you can overcome depression and anxiety, most of which you do not even have to pay for. So continue reading! Do not try to remember too much of the book yet! The solutions in the second half of the book are the important parts!

Chapter 1.3

Life for a depressed or anxious person

Up to this point, we were still answering the question: "What EXACTLY is Depression?" and we have learned many things about depression and its triggers. We also learned how the brain and body works in a person that is not depressed. We learnt the names of all the chemicals our body creates that influence our feelings. By now, you have probably decided it is worthwhile to overcome depression so that you may also experience the true happiness you long, and those feelings of safety and careless joy. So let us continue...

The last thing we need to discuss in this section is the emotions and thoughts we experience, that fall over like an unstable building.

We have already listed quite a few important things depressed people experience, like:

1. Sleep-depravation,
2. Constant tiredness and exhaustion,
3. Reduced hearing and vision,
4. No ability to concentrate and remember things,
5. Pain and headaches,
6. Severe stress,
7. Slowing down in thinking and reaction speed,
8. Not feeling in the mood to eat,
9. Losing interest in things you always enjoyed,
10. Becoming impotent,
11. Weaker muscles,

12. We have even touched those extremely sad or negative feelings that are constantly there…

Some other things depressed people may experience are:

1. Extreme gnashing of teeth during the day, and while sleeping,
2. A big struggle to study,
3. In some cases, ulcers all over the skin,
4. You may also experience body postures and gestures that change without the depressed person even noticing. This causes you to give unintended impressions to other people, like seeming irritated and angry while being calm, or the opposite. Sometimes a depressed person may be giving you the "cold shoulder", while they are actually trying their best to engage in their conversation with you.
5. Light-headedness and sometimes feeling horrible enough that you can only describe it as though it feels you are busy dying.
6. You talk a lot less, because you fail to concentrate and really think and remember the things you are hearing from others.
7. Some depressed people experience excessive crying, and most times, it is at night when the person can do it alone, though this is not the only time. Mostly this happens when the person is thinking about the overwhelming love they feel for others, but at other times, it may be for no reason at all. Another common reason is that the person feels overwhelmed by emotion.
8. Depressed individuals may constantly endure a sore body with muscles tightening around the neck, head, shoulders, and back.

    Many times a depressed person might catch these muscles clenching secretly, and then relax them. Sometimes, like in most anxiety-related cases of depression, these muscles will clench involuntarily, and the person finds it difficult to relax them.
9. Hormone production may also decrease in some rare cases of depression. Remember that one chemical imbalance will cause a whole chain-reaction of chemicals to be imbalanced in a depressed person. Your thyroid creates your hormones and it regulates your metabolic chemicals, and it is located inside your throat. Depression affects many of the hormone-glands in the thyroid. Did you know you could get your thyroid tested to be sure? Sometimes when depression attacks

your hormones, you may feel sexually attracted to the same sex! You know that is not you, but it is still there. This problem might also disappear when kicking depression out!

10. Another thing you may experience as a depressed person is leaving social groups for various reasons. You may become touchy-feely, and you think every gesture your friends are doing is to show you that they do not like you. This is a lie, but a depressed person believes these lies, and really thinks every one of those words is the truth. Why do depressed individuals believe these lies? Well, because the one person you trust the most is you yourself. Some depressed people also leave social groups because they feel weak and insecure about themselves. They fear their social group will throw them out, and so the depressed person will rather leave.

    There can be many other reasons too, but one of the most important ones is a feeling of resentment and rejection, that repeats itself a billion times a day. Depressed people do not choose to feel like this all the time and they cannot just "snap out of it", because an illness is causing these thoughts. If you have depression, you have to know that you can be as strong, quick, sharp, and fun as anyone else can! It only 'seems' as if your friends do not like you, but they really do! Why would they stick around if they did not? If you just get your chin up and find the glands in your body that is not working fast enough, and speed them up with medication or therapy, and various other things you will see later, you will start to see the satisfying truth you really want to see. The cool thing is that you do not even have to stay on the medication or therapy forever; that is if you even need it.

11. Eventually depressed people will start to participate in dangerous events, or they will over-expose themselves to addictions. This is because the adrenalin created by the dangerous event will make them feel temporarily better, and addictions numb our problems. The thing is adrenalin will not make us feel better for long, because it is not the root of the problem. Serotonin is.

    Addictions will not help us become better, because things like excessive daily alcohol, nicotine, and caffeine will attack and destroy the serotonin in our brain, causing us to forget our problems so we can have fun. However, forgetting the problem every day will not take the problem of too little serotonin away; it simply covers the problem and allows it to grow bigger and bigger behind the scenes.

You need to go to the root problem and fix the serotonin deficiency in your bloodstream with medication, or find freedom from your past with therapy if something is bothering you, before those thoughts create a serotonin deficiency.

12. The last thing that depressed people may experience is the most dangerous of all, and a big mistake! People with major depression sometimes experience suicidal thoughts, and may even fantasize or plan their own deaths. This should be watched closely by those around a depressed person, and even the depressed person themselves, because these thoughts can sometimes sneak up to you while your mind is running wild, and you don't even notice you think about it more often. It happens because a depressed person really does not feel happy inside.

The lack of serotonin will cause their bodies to stop producing all the "feel-good" chemicals they need. Over a period of time the person may feel heart-broken for no reason at all, and then the feelings of sadness stays there constantly and gets worse. The brain starts to expect the worst, because depression restructures thought patterns at this time. So you are always criticising yourself, feeling jealous of how others look or act, or for what they have, and many times these thoughts stay there for so long that it feels like the only way to have a break out of the craziness in your head is to force yourself dead... A therapist is there to restructure the neurons in your brain to think like a healthy person again.

They do it privately, and objectively, and they are a whole lot smarter than you think! They do amazing things that will make you laugh in amazement! Try it! You do not have anything to lose any way, do you?

Depression is an illness that causes you to feel hopeless, but you are actually worth a lot more than depression makes you think! Later in the book, you will see how you can relax these feelings. By the way, do you ever think of what you can become? You will amaze yourself! You do not have to think about something just because it jumped into your mind! Interrupt your thoughts even if you have to do it a thousand times a day, and think about positive things! Every morning when you wake up, you can say to yourself "Something good is going to happen to me!"

The way a depressed person thinks is quite different. A depressed or anxious person is not in a position to make big decisions, like selling a house, or changing a career. A depressed person, whether it be a man or a woman, is flooded with emotional thinking, not rational thinking. Try asking yourself this: Is the job causing your depression, or is the depression causing you to struggle doing your job? They very often criticise themselves because they do not feel self-worth. Others may think that there is no hope, and give up on caring about their lives and the things in it, and this is very understandable. The fact is there IS hope. I am going to surprise you to the point where you will not be able to contain it anymore!

We experience indescribable storms of racing thoughts repeating themselves in our minds, thinking about the worst things. Some examples are "I am not worth anything", "nothing will ever change", and "what if something happened to those I love so much"...

You may even think, "Will I survive", "I cannot do this", "I am tired", "nobody cares about me", "look at me", "I am so ugly", "I cannot do anything right", "why is life so unfair", "I will never have enough", "no one wants to feel sorry for me", "or help me", "no one's help is working", and many other things.

Sometimes these thoughts may repeat themselves in a depressed person millions of times a day, interrupting all their other thinking. It is crucial to know that this will cause less of the good chemicals in the body, but remember that a lack of exercise may also cause these chemicals to become less, and when we do not have enough of these chemicals, this may also induce the unnecessary thoughts that are so extremely hard to bear. So get yourself to see the glass half-full, and to be extremely positive. Do it on purpose, even if it does not work at first! Interrupt your thoughts! Adding some medication and therapy to the mix will help with this! Force yourself to be confident by sticking out your chest, and keeping your chin up, smile more and gym more. Take deep breaths! It is free!

A depressed person's feelings may also have been caused by a dramatic event in their past, and because they did not or could not mourn their loss, it is probably the worst thing to ever experience! This next description is solely for informational purposes.

What I want to do is to show you the feelings inside a depressed person. What you can do is to imagine yourself in these shoes.

Do not worry though, you will not feel bad the whole time; it is just going to be for a moment, so you can understand why a depressed person acts the way they do. A depressed person finds it difficult to describe how they are feeling sometimes. The problem is depressed people concentrate so hard to hide their depression, that they never remember their worst feelings while they are with others.

Most times when a depressed person wants to describe their feelings to someone, they always go home upset because they did not say everything they wanted to, but could not think about it all on the spot. The best way to describe the feelings of a depressed person is like this:

The last time you slept was 3 years ago... At the same time you have a heavy cold and flu, along with five other illnesses, and you are extremely nauseous and want to vomit really badly, but you do not have any medicine at all, and nowhere to go! You feel so exhausted, so fatigued, so much pain in your body, worn out completely, almost like there is no power in your body to pick up your arm...

Can you imagine your body feeling so weak, and so sick that you vomit when you stand up, but you have to pick up heavy things and pack it on high shelves all day? Your heart starts to beat so quickly and with so much pounding pressure that you can notice it, you're breathing faster, and then suddenly, after a few minutes, your heart goes so slow and soft it feels like it is going to stand still any moment, and you even forget to breathe. This feeling goes faster and slower the whole time.

It really feels like you are going to die any moment with all this happening and everything that is going crazy in your mind.

You cannot sleep but you crave a good night's rest as if you would exchange it with anything! You have lost everything you have, even your job, and you feel terribly sad and stressed about it. Now imagine you are sitting in the middle of hell, able to move but unable to run away while the devil himself pulls off all your toenails, and then goes to your skin, slowly tearing it off as you scream, and feel the terrible pain. I am not exaggerating about this.

While you feel like this the president tells his bodyguards to tie you up and to hit you until your whole body is blue, and feels dead, and to then shock and torture you, and to ultimately set you on fire while you are still alive, while you are standing on the edge of a sharp knife. While all this is happening, imagine you still have to try your hardest not to fall over your own feet because of the tiredness, and that you have to take all this with a smile as if nothing is wrong, or suffer the consequences of hell. Obviously, it is impossible to react to this with a smile.

Do you agree that this is quite horrible? This is just how their body feels, now comes the emotions:

You never feel in the mood for anything and anyone, you are always mad and upset with the biggest feeling of sadness in your heart ever, a sinking heart that is broken into a million pieces, and a throat that struggles to keep the tears in. Now imagine at the same time you had to lose all your best friends recently, all those whom you love to death, and they tell you that they hate you, but they do not know the truth about you.

What would it be like for you to lose everyone you love including your husband or wife, your children, your parents, or your brothers and sisters, and your best friends in a horrible torturing fire, even your favourite pet, or even something sentimental to you? Think about it! While all this is happening you still have to concentrate on the fact that your mother and father is telling you that they hate you with an absolute passion, and that you are worth absolutely nothing, a complete mistake, a stupid excuse for a person.

Everybody hates you. Now just bear with this please: While this is happening, everywhere you go someone says we wish you had never been born. It sometimes feels like even God has forsaken you, while all these tragedies are happening. The good news is He never leaves you! So anyway, these people laugh at you as you are getting sadder and sadder and you are so desperate to cry. Just think how it must be to feel like this every moment of every day, and every night, without stopping. If you can do that, you have just about seen 15% of how bad depression and anxiety really feels to someone suffering from it! This is a fact!

Someone suffering from depression or anxiety would really like to say something to the lines of this if someone asked them how they are really feeling inside.

You think YOU have problems. A depressed person feels like they have the stress of four very hard-working people at the same time, along with horrible sadness. Can you imagine how hard it must be for a depressed or anxious person to feel like this, and still cope with their real job and personal problems too? You do not know the beginning of depression yet!

Now I am not saying any of those things ever happened, and I certainly hope that none of it ever happens to any single human being, but this is the only way of knowing the EMOTIONS of a majorly depressed person. Most depressed people never even think this negatively, but their heart and body feels like all these things happened to them. The most interesting part of all is a depressed person does not always even have to think about ANYTHING for him or her to have these feelings, these heart-shredding, sad, sad feelings.

They can sit somewhere talking to their friends about what a great day they are having, and secretly feel this way the whole day. Now if you are depressed, for any reason, you have to know that, no matter what happened, there is hope, and you are worth a lot! There is a plan for your future, and YOU are actually a lot stronger than those people who never experienced depression.

You are feeling more pain than you should while you are mourning about a tragedy that only you would know really about, and it is all because of a chemical imbalance that catches up with you, and locks you in this place of turmoil. It is good to feel sad about things that happen in our lives sometimes, but none of us should stay stuck in our past, and if you think it is something more than just sadness you are experiencing, you can help yourself feel better. You just need to stand up and do something about it, even if you do not feel like it right now. You are the only person that can do something about your feelings

There is just one thing I want you to think about while you are fighting your depression, and that is, if you feel like you have to show people they are wrong about you; then do it only if you will live out your own life and dreams. Do not live toward anyone else's expectations and miss your own dreams!

This is everything we needed to discuss in answering the question of what depression really is, and next we can look at why depression happens.

Chapter 2.1

Some causes of depression

Well as you can imagine, depression has many different triggers! Countless things may be the cause of our body to imbalance its chemicals, but you have to remember that all forms of depression, anxiety, and even any form of illness, shows its symptoms because of something that disturbs our body's chemistry. No matter if it is physical, or simply a mental issue, they both may be the cause of the chemical instability in your body.

In other words, we may become depressed simply by what we choose to think about, or by some physical thing that happened in our past. Whatever the case, it is impossible to "just snap out" of it! It is something that we have to work out of our lives. The cause of our depression can be virtually anything, but the outcome will always be an important fluid in our bodies that is disturbed. So why does depression happen?

Well, as we learnt earlier, some general causes of depression are:

1. A traumatic event like an accident,
2. Losing loved ones, and friends, or even losing a job,
3. Failing in a specific field of study,
4. An operation on your body,
5. People who use you,
6. Your environment,
7. Medication with side-effects,
8. Stress,
9. A hard life as a child,

10. And some people can be born with depression,
11. While with others, it can be because of prolonged conflict at home.

There are many forms of depression, and if you have only gotten depressed recently, it is ok to wait and see if it will go away within a couple of months. It is only after two months that we know the depression is more serious, and we can do some things to try to get out of it, including sometimes seeing a therapist for a while to clear it up permanently. However, if you have had depression for a long time, it is a good idea to use the tips in this book to battle it properly the first time.

Have you ever noticed how quickly your emotions can go like a flip-flop up and down and up and down in an instant, just because you are listening to a specific song, or watching a specific movie, or even by being in the company of a specific person or group of people? Your emotions can also go rampant because you stay at home all the time and never get out and do something by yourself, or with someone.

Happy people are happy because they surround themselves with happy and uplifting things they enjoy, like partying, singing, dancing, best friends, many great visits, music, taking a break, enjoying their hobbies, and not being so stressed and rigid, and some people are even happy just because they don't allow people to use them, or walk all over them. That is why you are alive! You are alive to live! Learn to relax and laugh! It might be difficult in the beginning because your body will not immediately feel like doing these good things. Keeping it up for long enough though, especially in the very hard times, will make your body realign its chemicals and make you truly feeling happy.

Are you listening? Did you know breathing is free? Take deep breaths (breathe in), and relax (ahhhh)! Go out with friends, talk a lot, and just watch out for the occasional user who does not change. We cannot change people! We can simply ask and therefore, if someone is using you even after you had a talk with them, do what happy people do, and kick those people out. Do not allow them to poison your life.

Think about this: Do you have debt? Do you constantly think about it and roll it over in your mind every day? Does thinking about your debt get you out of debt? NO, it does not! So stop thinking about it! Simply stop spending until you can afford to spend! It is as simple as that! There is no way around this fact! Gain enough self-respect to say no to things you cannot afford. Pay your debt without thinking about it every day! It does not solve a thing to sit and stress about something you can only change slowly! Relax! Have a good time with your family and friends. If you enjoy an occasional "escape", then have some "you" time by the pool or outside.

Try getting in your car without dusting your feet first! Did you know that the word 'cleaning' exists in the dictionary so we can do it to dirty things? If you clean when there is nothing dirty, you are wasting your life! You do not have to live like a slob, but try to notice what a wonderful time you are having, instead of constantly looking at the little dust particle on your favourite shoes, or television screen! Use the things in your life! Make things dirty so that it can make sense when you clean them once a week! Learn to relax and just have a laugh! You do not need a reason to be happy! It is a simple choice! Smile!

Do not think yourself to death about what you're going to wear, what you're going to talk about, when you're going to clean your car, when you're going to make your bed, how many people saw that bad paint job, or what people think of you. Just forget about everything, do not care about mediocre things like that, and just have a party filled with smiles, jokes, and good talks with your friends while you are at work, or at home, or busy doing what you enjoy.

When you relax, you will notice how good you feel and how well you can start to think, because now your brain is not wasting all its serotonin to focus on the one thing that made you stressed. If you have a pressing problem, do not think about whose fault it is! Start thinking about solutions, and do not waste hours on the problem! After you have thought about it, put it out of your mind and do something you enjoy! You can think about it again later if you have to.

Then your brain can use its serotonin and other chemicals gently, as your mind is quiet and in a good mood, and clear without stress. It makes you feel like jumping and shouting, and laughing, and having fun, and having a refreshing drink with best friends and making exciting plans, feeling fulfilled with a sense of magic, and an especially strong bond with everyone you love, one that no one can break. Do you want this? Do you want this every day? Do you want to be free from depression? Well, read on so you may learn exercises, and diets, and all the other things you need to feel great!

The first thing you have to imprint into your mind is to stop caring about the dust, and the dirty water, and the smoke, and being filthy, and the smelly oil, and the dishes, and the time. Such is life! Locking yourself in a glass box is not going to make you happy! Just do not over-care about small things anymore! Yes, wash the dishes, but once a day, and clean your car, but do it once a week, and the rest of the time, forget it completely and have fun with those things. Do not get crazy when it gets dirty, because it will happen again, and again! If you expect visitors whose noses are always flying around high in the air, why would you want to spring-clean your house for them anyway? Do those irritating people deserve it?

Step grass into your car, get fingerprints all over the windows, let people chat and enjoy themselves in your car without telling them to clean their feet. Who cares? Only you care! You do not have to allow people to damage your things, but putting those things above your joy is not smart either. Do not live like a slob, but do not be a perfectionist either! Find the middle and you will do great!

Those things like your car is there to enjoy, and if you are stressing about everything, and not doing anything with your car but riding it like a boring person, you are not going to be happy.

You can stress about cleaning the car when it is Sunday and you have to clean it, but until then, relax about the dust, and the grass, and the dirty things, forget them completely and do not be shy to make some things dirty yourself without caring if you have to. Have fun while you are driving, watching a movie, or eating, or whatever. Are you upset about something? If you can fix that problem later, do it later! Do not think about it now!

If you want to relax in the sun, your towel does not have to be perfectly straight. If you are cold and can only get different coloured socks, wear them! It is fun! Really, try that one day, and like it on purpose! You will be surprised of what you can learn from different coloured socks! If you are really daring, show your socks to someone you know! You are not going to die if you do, and you might just have a fun conversation about them in the process! These things do not matter. No happy person cares about how well you can be a perfectionist. You are just killing yourself with stress! Yes of course uniform is uniform, but what are socks?

People think it lowers their standards when they have fun like this. Have you ever looked closely at those same people? Those people with "high standards" as they call it. They may seem rich, but they are not really, they might smile, or laugh, but they are not happy, and it is because they are not using the things they have! Some things will actually still exist after it got dirty, and you can really ease your mind and not even think about it until it is your scheduled time to clean it. You will not go down to a lower standard if you live carefree!

Standards mean to say things like "I won't settle for second best, I won't have a partner who is lazy, I won't have children until I am all set, I will not force my way to be done, and I will never interrupt other people". By the way, do not allow people to interrupt you either. Who cares if you have to show your anger when people walk all over you? Stand up for yourself calmly, but firmly, and you will only have to do it once. These things are standards, and they are the ones that make your life easier, and filled with joy.

Being carefree about the smaller things of life adds to this wonderful pleasure, and even God wants us to stop stressing, and have fun while we care for one another, and that is the only thing the Bible has to say about it. If you spring-clean your house when snot-wavers come to visit, you are allowing them to control you! Does it make sense? Of course it does! Being carefree about smaller things actually adds the biggest standard that exists to your life. If you are not enjoying yourself, and not making it happen with the biggest smile you have, you are going to have endless regrets when you reach 90 and you finally realised it. Make it happen!

Get busy, stop stressing about the amount of spit in your mouth, or about the unmade bed, and go out there and have fun with the people you love.

Now obviously we must be careful not to become slobs, making the bed gives us a little wake-up exercise, and brushing our teeth ensures our teeth stays in our mouth for longer, and washing your car will keep it good, but don't stress about these things excessively. Get them done, and relax and forget about them completely until it is the next time to get them done.

Do not stress about what you are going to say or talk about with people, just go and let them lead the conversation. This will give you a chance to listen, and to take over when you are ready about some interesting things you want to say. Tell people about what you have seen, or learnt, or about what your plans are for next month, or about anything that you do not have to plan a speech about before you get there. Just have fun. Believe it if you will, but your friends actually like you just the way you are! How do I know that? Well, because otherwise they would not have stuck around for long to become your friends in the first place.

Let us find out more about the process involved in overcoming your depression or anxiety in the next chapters.

Chapter 3.1

The process

We all wonder by now: "Where it all starts, and where it leads".

We have learnt so far that many things can trigger depression, and with every person, it can be a different form of depression. Sometimes, temporary depression can clear up on its own in two months or so. The most likely cause of this depression or anxiety is an external event somewhere in our lives, and as soon as the problem is gone, the depressive mood goes away. If the low mood stays for longer, it may be because the problem we are facing takes a bit longer to solve, and in many cases, a problem can find a way to stick with us for a longer period. In this case, if it seems like the problem is going to take longer to fix, the person can go for medication and therapy to help them feel better while facing this problem, which will in turn also keep them inspired to think on creative ideas for solving their situation. This often helps the solution to come sooner than it would have without treatment.

With other people, depression may be hiding in the closet for a long time, and only start to get worse later in their lives.

The point is if you have a depressed mood, or experience any of the symptoms mentioned in this book, you may ask yourself these questions: Is a stressful situation causing my sad or anxious mood? Do I need to do something about my situation before I will feel better? Should I wait for the solution to happen by itself? If I do something about my depressed mood, will it help me to solve the situation in my life better and quicker? Did I become my own happy self again when my circumstances got better? Have I been feeling unhappy or anxious for a long time without any reason? When will I feel better? Is it possible that I am feeling worse than I should, just because of a little gland in my body that is not creating enough chemicals for my brain? Am I simply diabetic, since the symptoms are so closely the same? Should I check up on this with my doctor?

I recommend that you ask yourself these questions, and then decide what you are going to do about it based on what you are going to learn in this book. There is no point in sitting around, blaming people, or blaming things, or just being unhappy the whole time, while depression is stealing your joy and your time!

Decide to do something about it! It might sound challenging, and you may definitely not be in the mood, but you have to stand up anyway! You will probably fall another thousand times, but standing up and being easy on yourself for a change is exactly what you need to do! It is not a good idea to think, "I can handle this depression or anxious mood", regardless of how small or insignificant your problem may seem. Go for gold!

Everyone will experience a slightly different path out of depression or anxiety. Basically, if the depression or anxiety has been around for longer than two months, the best thing to do would be to follow a healthier diet, and to exercise, to try and get better rest while not over-sleeping, and to go and have a nice comforting chat with a psychiatrist for some more detailed recommendations that will help you specifically. You only need one session!

This will help you know what type of depression or anxiety you are up against, and then the psychiatrist can tell you what to do! What do you have to lose? They really are cool people. It might take only a few weeks, or maybe it will take two years. You might need some medicine or therapy, or in some cases a you may need a combination of both, but working on it for a year and feeling great again, is much better than just sitting around and feeling bad forever.

Just remember to tell someone you can trust about everything. Having someone who can support you is a great idea, or even having someone whom can just listen and be there when you need to blow off some steam, decreases quite a bit of stress! Maybe you need someone who can run into the pharmacy for you, or do you a favour that you might need doing. You are going to be ok! Do not be so hard on yourself.

Really, do not think so badly of yourself. You are NOT all those bad things you think you are. Some people may be the best lions that they can be, but you have to be the best white-striped Siberian tiger YOU can be!

You really are much stronger, and much more of an amazing person than you may think right now. Just think of how much more you can become! Do not allow an illness to make you think different. You will learn better diets, and sleeping techniques, and exercise programs along with some therapy shortly, but before we look at the solutions, we are going to learn a little more about the medicine, the process, and some things you need to know to understand the solutions better in chapter four.

Chapter 4.1

Basics about the meds

You might be wondering when it will end in "happily ever after", am I right?

Well, that is something only a psychiatrist can tell you, because they are able to diagnose your type of depression, and tell you what you can do next along with all the tips in this book. Seeing a psychiatrist is not a weakness! Seeking help takes a very powerful first step, and not taking that step is not smart!

The point of medication and therapy is you get the medication to provide your body with enough serotonin, and then you start feeling better. This good mood will make it easier for you to go to the gym, and to see your therapist. These two things will both exercise the glands in your body that creates your "feel-good" chemicals. As soon as those glands have become stronger at making you feel better, you are ready to stop the medication and therapy, leaving you happy.

You will still feel sad when you have to, like any happy person, but you will not have depression any more, leaving you in a good mood more often, like with happy people. On very rare occasions, some anti-depressants may have withdrawal symptoms, or dangerous side effects, so it is important to tell the psychiatrist if you are using any other medications that may interfere with the anti-depressants so that she may prescribe the right one for you.

There are about twenty-five different types of anti-depressants, three of which are very popular. Let us have a look inside the brain again.

Think about the neurons, and the synapses between these neurons. Do you still remember that neurons are the "highways" where information travels on? Do you remember that synapses are the little open gaps between the neurons where that serotonin-chemical transports information safely from one highway to another?

Here is a quick summary for you on what to keep in mind from chapter one: When you think about something, electronic pulses will send the information from your memory to the tip of the first neuron. Here is serotonin, a chemical that captures that information in little balls. The serotonin "busses" will then safely travel through the synapse and into the second neuron-highway's tip where it can drop the information off. Then a second electronic pulse sends the information into a processor where you can "see" your thoughts. The serotonin will then return to the tip of the first neuron to wait for more information to send later.

Ok, now we can continue.

Here are three short examples of how anti-depressants work:

- The first category is normal anti-depressants. When your body is not creating enough of its own serotonin, this is the usual medication to use. What will happen when your brain does not have enough serotonin?

    An electrical signal will be sent through the first neuron, and then a weak chemical signal will be sent through the synapse because of too little serotonin, and then no electrical signal will go through the second neuron, causing all the symptoms of anxiety and depression. The main function of these anti-depressants is to provide your brain with more of this serotonin chemical.

    Keep in mind that it is possible to have very high levels of serotonin in your body, but you will still be depressed if you do not have enough GABA, which is the chemical that helps your body to absorb the serotonin! Do some research on GABA as a project to do some thinking on if you want to! You may read up on the physics of GABA yourself, as it is not a common problem in depressed people, but interesting if you want to know more about it! Have fun!

- SSRI's or Selective Serotonin Re-Uptake Inhibitors are the second form of anti-depressants. Remember, that after the serotonin has sent a message from one neuron into the second, it will come back to the original first neuron. Sometimes in any healthy brain, while you are busy thinking, some serotonin stays in the synapse (that little open gap) because it does not make it all the way through to the second neuron.

One of two things can happen to this serotonin. Either the first neuron can take the serotonin back (the re-uptake of serotonin), or the serotonin can be dissolved. Medication called SSRI's will block the first neuron from taking back the serotonin that was left in the synapse, forcing it to move further into the second neuron, or to be dissolved.

This increases the activity of the existing serotonin in the brain. Sometimes happy people may become temporarily depressed because of a pressing problem in their lives, and they might be over-thinking that situation. More serotonin dissolves every time we constantly ponder about the same thing, leaving us feeling depressed.

So if you have a problem that needs thinking, decide to take an hour of your time where there are no distractions, and to focus and try to think up a solution, and then do not constantly think about it after that hour. Plan a solution for the problem, and relax your mind during the rest of the day, because the less you think, the better you will feel, and the more ready your mind will be to do thinking when it really has to.

If you could not think of a solution in that hour, then make a plan to think about solutions again later, but until then, relax your mind and interrupt your thoughts with positive ones as much as you can! You will not become dumb if you think less! On the contrary, your brain will work allot better and be allot sharper if you do. Why is this, because you spare serotonin by thinking only when you need to!

- MAO's or Monoamine Oxidase Inhibitors are the last form of common anti-depressants. These anti-depressants will stop your brain from dissolving the serotonin that was left behind in the synapse, forcing the neurons to either send the left-behind serotonin all the way through to the second neuron, or to allow all the left-behind serotonin to be taken back by the first neuron. It prevents recycling, and in some depressed people, it works quite well!

Different medications will work for different people under specific conditions, so it is important to get the right one for your specific depression to be treated, and that is why you need a psychiatrist because they are qualified professionals in the field of medicine and depression. You might have heard of anti-depressant/anti-anxiety organic medicines, herbs, and teas that you may buy over the counter. Those also help, and it is ok to try them, but consider the stronger, more specific meds if these take too long or do not seem strong enough! Bet you cannot wait to see the solutions! Well they are all in one place so that you do not have to search long and hard for them later! It is coming so keep reading!

Just remember that your depression is curable, and that you can look and feel exactly as you want to! There is a way to do everything! Start to think outside the box! You just might come up with the best ideas to solve those secret questions you often ask yourself! I think you will surprise yourself! FINALLY, now that you know how depression and anxiety works, you can learn what you may do about it!

Chapter 5.1

The different types of depression

Ok, so here we are going to look at "How we get depressed, and how we can solve it?"

This is a very important question, because if we can find out where it all started in our own lives, we can better diagnose the type of depression we have, and solve it quickly and efficiently. There is just one little thing though... You are going to need someone to help you! There is no question about that!

What we are going to learn here in chapter five is:

1. What triggers depression in our lives.
2. What are the 15 different types of depression?
3. What we can do to overcome depression, specifically:

   a. What to do first,
   b. Who to see and when,
   c. What diet to follow,
   d. What gym program to be on, and
   e. Lastly, you will see some information on meditation and other categories.

We start by looking at the trigger of our own depression. What started it anyway? Any person on earth can get depression. There are many types of depression, and each type of depression causes us to think, act, and feel different. Every form of depression has a different duration. Some can take a lifetime to recover from, others last two years, and healing comes for some depressed people in a matter of weeks. It all depends on what caused the depression, and how long it took to notice we suffer from it, before we started doing something about it.

Mostly, when a loved-one passes away or leaves us, it tends to trigger depression. We can decide to mourn, or to ignore that fact. It is just too hard sometimes. As difficult as it is to hear, it is not healthy NOT to mourn. Others can get heavily depressed just from losing a job, or feeling insecure about their bodies, or failing a certain field of study. Some people get depressed after a traumatic event like a car crash. Medication that has a bad side effect can also cause depression. Did you know this?

We might even get depression from watching too much TV or using technology too often, rather than being active before and during our daytime. We may even stay depressed, just because we are depressed. This means that on rare occasion, the depressed person may have had depression for so long, that they actually fear getting better because it might change their beliefs and moral standards. This will not ever happen! Sometimes we disagree and fight with each other, and then we may lose very close friends.

People who stress a lot can also have their stress change into depression or a consciously anxious mood. There are even people who get depressed because of a hard life as a youngster. Many things can cause depression, at any time in our lives.

Sometimes people are born with depression. This means that a person is born with specific chemical glands that are too small, producing too little of a specific chemical needed to make the body feel good and happy. Then, if the child is not motivated to laugh a lot, and develop well in every area of life including making friends, exercising, trying new things, etc. the gland stays small and the problem is only noticed when the child grew a little older. Try to remember where you can see the symptoms of your depression for the first time, then think of everything that happened from then until today, so you can understand what type of depression developed in us, and fix it to regain the best life there is to live. I highly recommend that you write down everything you experienced from the first time you can remember your depression or anxiety started! Take a long time to think about it properly.

For example, in my case, I was born with depression, but I did not know this until I was 20 years old. Now I'm 24, and recently I thought back to try and see where my depression could have been noticed for the first time because I decided to record all my experiences to give to a therapist for a closer look at determining my type of depression.

I remember being tired and demotivated most of the time when I was younger, and I have an image in my mind of when I was around 7 years old, constantly feeling so tired that I was determined to be pushed in my pram the whole time, until my parents decided it is time for the pram to go. That is the first symptom, and then came all the other strange behaviour. I could never try new things or meet new people.

Look at your entire past, and try to see the first visible part that could have meant depression, and try to remember everything that happened from then on, so that you and your therapist can use that information in determining your solution to feeling better again. Here are all the most common types of depression, and its symptoms. Have a look at them, and see if you can spot the one or two that describes your situation the closest.

1. First we get Major Depressive Disorder (which is also known as Major Depression, or Clinical Depression) – Its symptoms last for at least two weeks at a time, and with maximum depressed mood and no interest or pleasure in any activities you once enjoyed. Other symptoms are:
   Change in weight and appetite, difficulty sleeping, excessive movement or slowing down quite a lot mentally and physically, no energy, feeling worthless and very guilty without reason, difficulty thinking, concentrating and making decisions, and often thinking about death or suicide.

2. Secondly, there is Dysthymic Disorder (or also named Dysthymia) – This causes a nearly constant depressed mood for at least 2 years with some of the following symptoms:
   Change in weight and appetite, difficulty sleeping, low energy, very low self-esteem, difficulty concentrating and making decisions, and feeling hopeless. These symptoms do not occur for more than two months at a time. This form of depression is very persistent but less severe than Major Depression.

3. Manic Depression (or now known as Bipolar Disorder) – Is a kind of depression that includes periods of mania and depression. What do these words mean? Read on to find out! Bipolar disorder means the

person's emotions will be cycling between these two states, like two different personalities and it can change rapidly. In some cases, the cycles between mania and depression may take months or even years, or only mania can be present the whole time without any depressive episodes.

When the person is in the manic state, he will have a very elevated or irritable mood that is extreme. When this manic state is over, the depressed state starts, feeling slowed down and sad, and the person will constantly bounce between these two states until the person gets medication for the problem.

Unfortunately, there have not yet been any recorded cure for bipolar disorder, and for some other types of depression like schizophrenia, but they are completely manageable.

It is generally long-term, but I believe it must also be permanently curable, because the switching in these two states must be triggered by something like sounds or events, and some people can be hypersensitive to certain sounds and events triggering adrenalin production in the body, which can be the cause for triggering mania in bipolar disorder. Here is a practical example to understand it better! There have been recorded cases of people getting epileptic seizures during a day at the zoo! Researchers have proven that it is because of the roaring sounds of lions and tigers. Their noises are at the specific frequency required to trigger a seizure in some epileptic patients! The same thing may also happen in bipolar patients! Certain sounds, smells, or images can also induce the rapid change in their mood!

However, it is important to remember that bipolar patients can also have a change in their mood without any trigger! This is the norm!

Bipolar patients that are not on the meds cannot help it when their mood changes dramatically like this! When they are on the meds, and their mood goes from depressed to happy, they often feel the need to stop the meds, because they believe it is not necessary any more. Watch out for this closely! Always take the meds, and your mood will always be a little bit less agitated. Anyway, if you can take away the hypersensitivity in the brain by exercising the other chemical glands in the body, then the mood changes might be a little bit more stable. Then the chain-reaction of unstable chemicals might be broken. Some brain-exercise may also be required to make the brain less sensitive to events, by making the brain more used to these events.

By exposing yourself to these events in a controlled fashion with the help of a therapist, you will be able to perform this exercise. They do not do this by default, but might try it with you if you suggest it!

Some of these symptoms are also present in bipolar patients, especially in the manic state: Very high self-esteem or self-importance, almost no need to sleep, very excessive talking and many racing thoughts and ideas! They get very easily distracted, get very busy, and move around a lot. In this manic state, they also expose themselves to very excessive involvement in risky but pleasurable behaviour like over-spending, careless sexual activity, and unwise business investments. When the depressed state starts, they experience a very intense major depressive episode like the first type of depression in this list.

These symptoms can be severe enough to warrant hospitalization to prevent harm to self or others and it can sometimes include psychotic features like hallucinations and delusions. This means the person can experience voices talking to them, or see things that no one else sees or hears.

If you have a psychological problem like this, there are people out there who understand. There ARE answers. Use medication, and if you want to, you can devote your entire life in finding a cure. Have you ever thought of all the good things that will happen if you manage to find a cure? Maybe trying all the advice following in this book is a good start.

You are an important person. You do not have to give up. Just remember to keep searching for a cure when you are in the happier state of your emotions too! However, use the medications that manage this depression in the meantime.

It is not that bad, and then you do not have to jump between these cycles anymore. Most bipolar individuals like to stop taking their medication while they are in the manic state because they feel healed, but it is not a good idea.

Other types of depressive categories are:

4.   Post-Partum Depression or "after-labour depression". This is almost always a temporary situation, and is experienced by mothers who give birth. Post-Partum Depression tends to be very intense. It starts roughly a couple of weeks after the child is born, and is different for every mother. Some women take longer than others to recover and they all experience diverse levels of "force" on their emotions from it. Don't wait to treat this issue. Don't let it eat away at you or your child or family members. There are people out there who love and care about you, and they might just surprise you if you were to ask for their support. Do the right thing... The honourable thing... For your child and for yourself. Ask for help. Take courage and ask for help.

5.   Have you ever heard of SAD or Seasonal Affective Disorder? The symptoms of SAD are the same as that of major depression. The feelings of distress are also relatively persistent and strong, but interestingly though; those who suffer from this condition will only experience episodes of distress in specific seasons, like winter or autumn. SAD is not a constant depression, and is therefore called Seasonal. Do you know someone who may be suffering from this curable problem? Perhaps the best way you could help them is by helping them identify the problem, by showing them this book.

6.   And then we get a condition known as Anxiety Depression. If you haven't realized this yet, there's a very big difference between anxiety and depression. And also between stress and tiredness, more of which you'll learn here soon. Anxiety Depression (or anxious sadness perhaps) is a disorder in which a stressful and anxious feeling or trail of thought will be present along with depression. Panic attacks and social phobia are normal conditions that are usually caused by, or linked to this psychological issue, and is also treatable. Don't think that you're alone. Never give up! To name a few, Generalized Anxiety Disorder and Post-Traumatic Stress Disorder (re-occurring stress after a big and stressful event) are also linked to Anxiety Depression. Speak to your family doctor immediately! They have answers!

7.   As we've learnt earlier, major depression and dysthymia are relatively harsh conditions, both of which can be overcome. Another variation of these depressive conditions is called Atypical Depression or "Unusual

Depression". Patients will experience excessive weight gain and a strange heavy feeling in the arms and legs, due to always feeling peckish or hungry. Patients of this depression do not handle rejection well at all, and the enormous stresses that these people usually experience will always leave them feeling tired and sleepy, being one of the major causes for many people to lose interest in their hobbies.

8. Can you believe that there's even such a thing as <u>Chronic Depression</u>, or "lasting depression"? This is not a permanent depression, but is definitely one that lasts around 2 years, and is usually severe as severe as Major Depression.

9. <u>Double Depression</u> on the other hand, is a combination of two specific types of depression. Most commonly found, patients of this depression experience chronic dysthymia (which is a mild depression), and then together with this, a temporary (usually roughly two weeks in duration), severe major depression. Have a look at the symptoms of Major depression and Dysthymia. Do you fit the bill here? Remember that no grip should ever be able to hold you down, if you don't let it. Do something constructive about it. Having these depressive symptoms are tiring, and you may not feel like fighting, but that's the exact moment you have to jump up, and say: "The buck stops here!"

10. Next we come to a psychological state which is surprisingly easy to diagnose, but very difficult to treat. It's called <u>Endogenous Depression</u>. This one means "depression from within the body". Have you ever felt depressed for no reason at all? Just down and out, experiencing lots of blue Mondays in a row? That's exactly what this is. If you are depressed for no reason at all, you may be experiencing this fixable issue. Again I reiterate: Go and visit your doctor! It can't do any harm! The only harm a person can do to himself is the harm of not taking action. This depressive state will come and go, and for some people it takes longer to overcome than others. Not everyone even experiences the same intensity of feelings or stress with this depression, so you can see why it's so difficult to treat. Doctors have to just take it one step at a time and you too!

11. Perhaps one of the most common types of depression, which is regularly experienced by almost everyone alive today, is <u>Situational Depression</u>. In a day and age where life tends to disappoint us regularly, this

depression roams wild and free. It's a depressive or stressful time which a person goes through, in relation to specific events that happen to us in real time, and can also be called Reactive Depression. It's a depressed mood which is experienced by patients who suffer from Adjustment disorder. Have you ever experienced weakness in maintaining healthy relationships with your loved ones, or have you ever had difficulties performing your duties at work or school, for a short period of time, because of something stressful that may have happened to you in that time? You're getting hot then! Symptoms of this depression start showing in less than 3 months of the stressful event, and tends to not last longer than about 6 months. It is definitely an intense form of stress, but because of its sudden nature, it is not within the same criteria as major depression.

12. Another form of depression which falls within the category of major depressive disorders is called <u>Agitated Depression</u>. Have you ever gone through a time where you are generally irritated all the time, and can't seem to fall asleep at night? Then you may be suffering from Agitated depression, and should seek an opinion from your doctor. Tiredness and forgetfulness are usually also symptoms here, because of the lack of sleep, not to mention "sluggishness" which one constantly feels while being tormented in this way. If you feel relatively irritated at everything and everyone, for no apparent reason, don't overlook this. In doing so, you're only neglecting yourself and your own health. It's not worth it to waste all your precious time on being irritated, where you could be laughing or spending time with loved-ones, being happy and doing the things you enjoy. Your health is important, and by the way, you don't want those grey hairs popping up any sooner, or the likelihood of your bones to break easier, just because your stress-chemicals are eating you up from the inside, do you?

13. Now it's worth mentioning another, more serious type of depression, which is known as <u>Psychotic Depression</u>. Sufferers of this condition experience depression as well as psychotic symptoms. They can see or hear things that do not exist, or often put their belief in things which are not true. Believe that this is also a treatable condition. You do not have to suffer from this discomfort. Luckily people who suffer from this state of mind only suffer from the initial experiences of

hallucinations, which come and go. There can be differences in the intensity of such experiences though, and it is imperatively important that you visit a doctor for them to do a proper analysis, and give you their recommendations.

14. <u>Melancholic Depression</u> is a type of depression in which a person will lose pleasure in hobbies, and their mood also does not improve at all when they are introduced to positive news or events. Almost like just giving up on everything, just going through the motions. The specific depressive mood that a person experiences here is very different from normal depressions or grieving. Melancholic Depression is consistently worse in the morning. It also causes you to wake up much earlier than usual, so tiredness and forgetfulness is sure to be sub-symptoms. Sufferers generally don't want to eat much, and always blame themselves for everything that goes wrong around them. They also tend to be restless, moving around a lot, and seeming distracted on a regular basis. Don't waste your time, get diagnosed. Get treated!

15. <u>Catatonic Depression</u> is another type of major depression, and is also known as "Unresponsive Depression". This is a serious condition, and it is VERY important to know how to respond to people who suffer from this crippling condition. Sufferers will lose control of their own movement. It's not by choice at all. They will just lose the ability to control themselves, and in most common cases they will become unable to react to their surroundings. At other times they will become aggressive or move excessively. All those who experience Catatonic Depression will clash with those around them, and avoid instructions from other people. Catatonic patients become unable to speak at times, and at other times may choose to stop talking. They also behave strangely in the sense that their movements become bizarre or repetitive. Have your attention ever been drawn to someone who has strange facial expressions, or who repeat what others are saying around them? Some catatonic patients also copy the movements of others around them, even if it does not make any sense, and they have no control over these actions. It is highly recommended that the family and friends of such a person be made known of the condition, so that they may avoid becoming offended for inappropriate things these patients may do or say, and these sufferers must visit a doctor to get

the problem treated as soon as possible. If it may be you, don't waste any more time. Don't give up! See your doctor or therapist, or even your local church and get involved. Get to a place where you can be supported and helped. You don't have to stay where you are!

These were the most common types of depression, and determining the right one you are struggling with is very important in solving the problem! Keep in mind that you can highlight the symptoms you experience, and ask a therapist to help you look at them and determine your type of depression or anxiety. Now just remember, if you start feeling better after doing some things to overcome depression do not stop!

You have to continue in a pattern for at least two years to take severe depression away. It may go quicker, but a psychiatrist will tell you the time you need. You do not want to stop and fall straight back to where you were! Sometimes it is too difficult to see which variation of depression someone has, and in this case, if medication is required, the medication may be tested and changed until the best one for you is found. You do not have to do it forever, but let the psychiatrist decide when you are ready to stop.

Chapter 5.2

Important solutions for depression

This brings us to the last part of our fifth and final question: How can we solve depression?

Actually, there is quite a lot you can do to free yourself of depression, so let us start discussing these things, but before we do, there is one more thing you need to know. Throughout this section, I will be talking about psychiatrists and therapists often, and it is important for you to know the difference.

- A psychiatrist is fully qualified and registered in therapy AND medicine. This means they can accurately diagnose your type of depression, and then prescribe the right medicine to help your depression go away. We always see a psychiatrist first, to get started on medicine before we go for therapy. A psychiatrist will also monitor what the medicine is doing to you once every 2 months, and he will adjust the strength of the medicine, as you need it.
- A therapist also studies medicine, but their profession is therapy, meaning they are just as qualified, but just not registered to prescribe medicine to patients, because they give therapy. A therapist is a person we see once a week after we started taking anti-depressant medication from a psychiatrist.

    They are the people we talk with, so they can help us think and feel better, and understand our emotions. Do not ever think you understand your emotions on your own, because these people can help and astound you in the most amazing ways to describe!

- These people are professionals, and they always work together when helping you, even if they never knew each other before. Once every week your psychiatrist will call your therapist and then they will brainstorm and talk about your progress, and decide on what to adjust. They actually have to do this! Since the psychiatrist is the first person we see, he will always have many therapists that he can refer you to, but you may also choose to go to your own therapist.

- To summarize, a psychiatrist can prescribe medicine for depression, and a therapist can help with your thinking patterns while you are on the medication.

- Something to keep in mind: Therapists do not need to have gone through terrible situations before they can understand you. They have studied for quite some time, and they are qualified in pressing the buttons in our brain that will help our brain restructure its thinking to how it is supposed to be. They help you to help yourself. They know exactly which buttons to press, and how to do that by talking to you. I never thought seeing a therapist could make such a big difference, but when I went, I was amazed at how they can really "talk" you better!

I was flabbergasted to notice how they help you change your thinking, and allow your body to realign its chemical thinking to how it is supposed to be. They can even show you sleeping and concentration techniques you can use while you are still fighting the depression. You see, the medication from the psychiatrist will numb your depression, while the therapy from the therapist will help you fix the problem, and when you are ready, the therapist and psychiatrist will decide that it is safe for you to go off the medication and keep on feeling good. Mostly, depression takes any time from two weeks to two years to heal, but if it is not caught early, and monitored closely, it can become chronic depression, meaning it may take a lot longer to heal from the depression, a potentially life-long use of medicine, so do not waste any time.

Let us start talking about the things we can do to solve our depression. These first three things are the most important ones to do, but if you think it is not a major problem, and you want to try solving it on your own first, you will see those extra tips and tricks shortly! You can even do them while you are seeing your therapist! Enjoy these next parts!

1. The first step is to tell someone you may have depression. Having depression is not a weakness at all. On the contrary, it takes real character to be able to cope with depression, especially if it is long-term depression, and it takes a very strong person to tell someone about your depression. Would you apologize if you were a diabetic? OF COURSE, YOU WILL NOT! Depression is an illness! Having someone to talk to about it really helps you to push off some steam inside you, and you can do it as often as you need to. This will also give you some new and creative ideas and motivation to do what you have to do.

2. Secondly, you have to feel confident that you have an accurate diagnosis of your type of depression. Remember, there is a difference between being sad for a long time, and having depression, so making sure you do in fact have depression to start with, is important. You can do this by searching for some free depression tests that on the internet, and after answering a few of them, you can go to a psychiatrist so that he can do his certified 15 minute test on you just to be sure. It takes 15 minutes at the most, and it is very affordable to see one.

    Borrow money if you have limited finances. Borrow your neighbour's internet if you do not have access at home. Just make sure you answer the questions truthfully, because if you fail to answer exactly how you feel, then the test results will not be accurate, causing you to use the wrong medication for your depression. They will prescribe medicine for you only if you need it. To contact a psychiatrist, you can look for any medical aid number in the phone book.

    If you call and ask them, they will send you a list of contact details for all the psychiatrists in your area via e-mail! Do it, even if you do not feel like it right now! You can even look on the internet for someone, maybe call directory enquiries. Their South-African number is 1023. It is free! You can even go to any normal doctor or hospital for a reference to a psychiatrist near you. Just remember, medicine will not always take away the negative thoughts on its own! It will lift your mood slightly, but after getting the medication, you have to move to step three.

3. Step 3 is to go and see a therapist for a while. If you use the medicine without seeing a therapist, you might feel worse because the medication will enable you to think more as well, allowing an overflow of negative thoughts if you do not see a therapist to help with your thinking patterns. They will also teach you the most amazing things, like techniques that healthy people use to feel good, or to sleep and concentrate better.

    They may only practice therapy if they are fully qualified, because if they cause someone's death, they can get into huge trouble. These people do not play around; they really know what they are doing. You can find their contact details in the same way as is described in step two. This is also very important, if you just cannot pay for the medicine, you must still see a free therapist at least because it is a good start to fighting your depression, and it will still help. Your doctor may have contact details for free counselling, and so do some churches. In the last chapter of this book, you will see the contact details of a therapist who offers free services or donations if you are able and you want to call her.

Chapter 5.3

Your diet

Here are some other very important things you can do to overcome your depression, and they are important to do while you are seeing a therapist. It will make your immune system strong against fighting this depression, but if you cannot see a therapist yet, you can start with these in the meantime. Remember, it is a mental thing, but also a physical thing, and one of these caused the other. So what other things can you do to help overcome your depression?

A good start would be to upgrade your diet. Think about this, your body needs specific vitamins to create serotonin, adrenalin, dopamine and all the other feel-good chemicals, but if you do not eat the vitamins that your body uses to create these good chemicals, your body will of course create less, leaving you with a bad mood! How do you think your body can make you happy if you do not give it the fuel it needs to do it? You also need to cut out the things that help create bad chemicals in your body. Some people have gout and some are diabetic and cannot adjust their eating habits to everything mentioned here, but they can just leave out some of these specific food groups. You can also consult your doctor to check these foods and tell you which ones you should skip before changing your diet if you have a medical condition.

Make these foods the number one thing in your diet. In addition, make a weekly plan you can use to eat all these foods. Just do not EVER leave your stomach hungry!

Try to eat six small meals every day, rather than only one or two big meals a day. Spread your daily eating times evenly throughout the day, however, try to eat your last meal at least an hour before going to bed. This diet is not going to work if you do not make the effort of writing it down, and making a 7-day plan for yourself!

Before you learn about these foods, you have to know this: Your doctor can perform five important tests to determine if a bad diet is what is causing the depression! These tests are a full blood panel, a thyroid test making sure to check T (3), T (4), and TSH, a urinalysis, a cytotoxic blood test and a hair and nail analysis.

If you cannot go for these tests, do not stress. You can still follow a healthier diet anyway to start with. Now have a look at the good foods you can use for a better mood. Try to get at least 90% of these foods in your weekly diet! The cool thing about these foods is, they are all very healthy, and you can have as much of them as you like!

Here are good foods and drinks that fight against depression and anxiety:

o   Fresh fish like (herring, pink salmon, tuna, mackerel, and even sardines) helps serotonin production. They even help your brain by making it easier for serotonin to move around in your brain. The omega-3 fatty acid in fish aids a better mood very well! This oil is an amazing one that can help with so many things like faster thinking, and it even helps cure or relieve arthritis! Research this oil to see what else it heals! It is also important for normal brain function, and aids a healthy heart. Did you know it even avoids strokes and heart attacks? Omega-6 fatty acids are also very important to ingest, and it is available in fish, nuts, seeds, and certain oils! You should try to use these oils in a ratio of 2:1, ingesting more of the omega-3 oil. Sources of these two omega-oils are also found in olive oil (this is the king of cooking oil), flaxseed (or linseed), and walnuts. Try adding walnuts to a tuna salad!

We need to eat omega-oils every day! Being low in these oils can decrease your sex-drive quite a bit, it can induce suicidal thoughts or anxiety, make you feel sad, and low omega levels even cause sleeping problems! Remember though, to avoid large fish, farmed fish, or any fish that is high in mercury or other toxins! You can buy books on these fish or research them on the internet! Toxins are serious things to avoid because it can cause many diseases in humans, or cause heart problems and high blood pressure!

It may even cause a permanent problem with short-term memory! Eat young, healthy fish types like those mentioned above, and avoid high levels of toxins!

Fish like barracuda, shark, swordfish, king mackerel, large marlin, yellow-fin tuna, sea bass, and many others are high in toxins! Avoid these! If you research the topic, you will find that these fishes are high in toxins because of our own environmental air and water pollution! Another thing to remember is that cooking these fish will not kill the toxins! The right fish is very important to eat almost every day! Do not forget about the olive oil and walnuts! You can eat a handful of walnuts every day, and you can cook with olive oil every day!

o   Healthy carbohydrates like (whole grain wheat bread, crackers, pasta, and oat cereal). Remember, low carbohydrates means low mood. Eat healthy carbs, because it helps serotonin production, it gives our body energy and power, helps us from over-eating, and it stops us from feeling down and slow by cleaning our bodies. Eating the wrong carbs, like too much chicken, or potatoes, or fatty meat will leave you feeling hungry even if your stomach is full!

This is because the wrong carbs do not create enough serotonin, so your brain cannot shut down your appetite after eating! Chicken and potatoes are not bad for your body, but too much of them are not healthy either. When your body craves something, it is not in your control! Your brain tells you when you are low in something, and it is in control! So eating the right healthy carbs will help you greatly.

o   Fresh fruits including (citrus fruits, banana, pomegranate, apple, pineapple, and blueberries) help a low mood become better. They contain mountains of healthy nutrients, dietary fibre, and anti-oxidants! There are other fruits like avocado, and guava, which will also stimulate serotonin production. The key ingredient in fruit that helps serotonin production is tryptophan. Research other foods high in tryptophan for a wider variety of fruit that you can turn into a daily smoothie!

o   Fresh vegetables like (beans, peas, carrots, and tomatoes), because being low on these healthy vegetables also lowers mood. Vegetables, like fruit, are also high in tryptophan. Your body also needs vegetables for a healthier diet that will improve your body's vitality, and restore a better mood. It also contains very important anti-oxidants and nutrients. Eating these daily will not only be healthier, and it will not only leave you in a more upbeat mood, but it will also regulate your weight and cholesterol levels much better if you prepare them healthily.

o   Garlic is very healthy, and it has a slight mood-elevating effect. Eat one clove of fresh chopped garlic every day.

o   Tryptophan is an amino acid that can relieve depression. Your body uses tryptophan to make serotonin! You may find it in (turkey, chicken, fish, peas, nuts, sunflower seeds, pumpkin seeds, fruits, vegetables, and peanut butter). Eat these foods with a healthy portion of carbohydrates like (whole wheat bread, potatoes, pasta and rice), and it will help your brain to take up the tryptophan in your stomach.

Do you see this? Turkey contains tryptophan. Pasta helps your body to use this tryptophan! Mix these foods for a healthy plate and remember to cook them with olive oil! It is very important to use a variety of all the foods mentioned in this diet plan, because of the brain-blood barrier! Sometimes you may eat foods that are high in serotonin production, but it does not always make it through to your brain. This is because serotonin needs amino acids like tryptophan to help the serotonin to cross the brain-blood barrier. You also need other amino acids to be levelled, and not too high, so that they do not take up too much space in this barrier. Have variety in your foods, but keep tryptophan in mind!

o   You can heavily add spices like (cayenne pepper, rosemary, ginger, cardamom, and basil) to your dishes. These herbs will help your body to create more serotonin for your brain, and it will help your brain to use this new serotonin more effectively. You can use these spices very heavily every day!

o   Drink mountains of fresh water. Every time you go to the toilet, you can remember to fill your body with water again. However, you really have to force that water down as much as you can get back in without feeling uncomfortable, and soon you will start to love it. Water helps your body to stay clean. It rinses your liver and kidneys, preventing toxins to build up too high in your blood. It helps you to lose weight, it makes a person more alert, and it helps your body to digest food! Water even helps your body to recover quicker from different parts swelling! Water even helps your body to use that all-important tryptophan more productively.

o   Also, drink a lot of freshly squeezed lemon juice, every day! If you do not like lemon juice, you can replace this with grapefruit or fresh orange juice. Use them often! At least one glass a day!

o   Earl-Grey black sugar-free tea is also a mood enhancer.

o   At the grocery store, you can find many anti-depressant herbal teas, like (peppermint, lemon balm, and ginger). They are also available at almost all pharmacies. Melissa herbal teas help with depression, minor sleep problems, and nervousness. Lemon balm tea has a calming, relaxing effect and reduces hyperactivity and being irritated, but use this one only twice a week at most as continuous use may reduce hormonal activity of the sex glands. Peppermint tea stimulates all brain functions, makes the brain feel ready for a challenge, and helps with clear thinking. These are very healthy even on the long term.

o   There are many scented anti-depressant oils, and you can mix them into your food, butter, milkshakes, and other dishes every day, like bergamot, neroli, rose, mandarin, lemon, lime, orange, cardamom, and rose oil. These are all healthy! Go on the internet to find interesting ways to mix healthy amounts of these oils into your food and drinks. Mostly, one to five drops every day in a milkshake or in your food would do the trick. You can even mix your butter with a few drops of these oils!

o   Monitor your use of sugar carefully, because too much sugar makes it difficult for your brain to have a strong memory, and too little sugar causes mood swings. Too much unhealthy cooking oil, butter and too much unhealthy fat in your diet is also a bad idea, because they all cause you to feel tired, and to struggle with memory. Use them sparingly, but do not stop using sugar! If you are diabetic, of course you have a replacement for sugar!

These were the most important foods we need every day, not just to improve our mood, but to stay healthy! Let us look at these foods in a short, summarized way now before continuing. You will notice in this summary the good foods, and the vitamins and nutrients they contain. Remember these nutrients, or write them down, so you can check other foods for these vitamins also.

The five best foods for fighting depression are:

1. Firstly, fish oils, because they contain healthy omega-3 fatty acids. These are extremely healthy for the brain. Just a gram of this oil daily may quickly decrease depression symptoms such as anxiety, sleep disorders, the sometimes-unexplained feeling of sadness, suicidal thoughts, and even decreased sex drive by as much as 50%. You can get these healthy oils in walnuts and oily fish like salmon and tuna. These oils will even lower cholesterol in your blood. Yes, some oils are actually healthy and good for you!

2. Then we get brown rice. It contains vitamins B1 and B3, and folic acid. It also releases a lot of glucose into your bloodstream, preventing sugar lows and mood swings. Your brain runs on glucose, but check with your doctor first about how much to eat every day if you are diabetic! Brown rice helps lower cholesterol, and it makes it easier for our body to extract important minerals and vitamins out of other foods.

3. Brewer's yeast contains vitamins B1, B2, and B3. It also contains 16 different amino acids, and 14 minerals. It actually contains mountains of good properties in small little packs, and adding a pinch of brewer's yeast to your daily food is a great anti-depressant. Just be sure your body tolerates yeast well, otherwise you can skip this one.

4. Whole-grain oats has folic acid, and pantothenic acid, which is vitamin B3, along with vitamins B1 and B6. It also lowers cholesterol, helps us digest food better, and can help with sugar levels, meaning it also helps take mood swings and an irritated mood away. It is always a good idea to replace white flour foods with whole-grain foods.

    Here is the rule: The whiter the bread, the quicker you are dead! Remove all the good nutrients and oils in brown bread and you get a longer lasting white bread for a longer shelf life in shops! This means you are actually eating air when you use white flour foods! White flour does not kill you, but it fills you up and prevents you from getting all the nutrients your body needs every day! This is not such a good idea.

5. Cabbage is also very important for depressed people: Cabbage contains vitamin C and folic acid. These vitamins protect us against stress, infection, cancer, and heart disease. If you would like to avoid gas after eating cabbage, you can add some fennel seeds, or cumin seeds to the dish. It is also great at stabilizing blood sugar. Did you know it even cures stomach ulcers? Cabbage is amazing stuff!
6. Other great anti-depressant foods are raw cacao, dark molasses, and Brazil nuts. These foods are great at boosting brain function and eliminating depression.

Now if you cannot adapt to this diet, there is still good news! You can go to a pharmacy and buy these vitamins in one tablet! It is still 100% with no side effects, and it is completely healthy! Go to your nearest pharmacy and buy the strongest vitamin supplement you can find, but check out the ingredients! It should not contain caffeine or ephedrine, or any other strong energy booster! It must be pure vitamins, and you can ask your pharmacist about this. You want concentrated vitamins, not a concentrated energy booster.

Also, buy the strongest anti-oxidants you can find. Vitamins and anti-oxidants are the two healthy tablets doctors use every day not to get sick while working with all those ill patients. It has no side effects if you use it often. Vitamins are not too expensive, and you can use them every day, with your normal diet. You can even use them with anti-depressant medication.

You need omega-3 and omega-6 fatty acids, vitamin B1, B2, B3 or pantothenic acid, B5, B6, B12, biotin, folic acid, tryptophan and vitamin C to help your body generate and use its own anti-depressants effectively. If you use these supplements, you must still drink enough water and try to avoid unhealthy oils and foods though! However, if you have major depression, it would be a good idea to see a psychiatrist also, as this diet may only take 60% of the depression away in such a case, and not heal it completely.

Here are some bad foods and drinks you should try to avoid:

a. All forms of caffeine including (coffee, normal tea, and cola) because it stops your body from creating serotonin, and it even prohibits your body from using the serotonin-foods you eat properly! Did you know normal tea and cola both contain caffeine? Caffeine is evil stuff for depressed and anxious people. It may cause long-term problems!

b. "Instant" foods, is a very bad idea, and fast foods should not be eaten too often. They are high in unhealthy oils! This is poison!

c. It is very important to use alcohol sparingly, because it is actually a depressant itself! It does a lot more than to just numb your nervous system; it attacks serotonin in the body, dissolving it. Alcohol will also damage certain receptors in your brain, doing permanent brain damage! That is why you hear that you lose brain fluid every time you go to the toilet after drinking alcohol.

   It temporarily enhances your mood, only because you do not feel the problem anymore! It does not take the problem away! Alcohol allows the problem to grow bigger behind the scenes! Alcohol takes away a very important vitamin from your brain, called thiamine or vitamin B1, and it is important for normal brain function.

   Your body also needs to fight against the alcohol so you can sober up, and it does this by releasing certain enzymes in your body that can remove the alcohol. This means that the nutrients your brain could have used, is gone thanks to alcohol, leaving you with a heavy hangover! It is ok for people to use alcohol sparingly on occasion, but a depressed person should use it very sparingly, or avoid it completely.

d. Nicotine is also very bad for people with depression, because nicotine is a depressant as well, just like alcohol. Smoking will have the same effect on a depressed person as alcohol. It lifts your mood for the first few months, but then the smoking will not help improve your mood anymore, and then the depression will be worse than before. So do not start. It also damages neurons and receptors in the brain along with its chemicals, and can permanently slow down your body from creating certain chemicals! That is why heavy smokers become impotent, or sterile! It is because your chemical-glands also damage through alcohol and nicotine use!

   If you did start however, try to stop, even if it is difficult. Retry and retry until you succeed. Do whatever it takes! The pills and patches really help! Any drugs are a bad idea for a depressed person, but for normal people too, because it decreases the chemicals our brain needs to think and regulate everything in your body to keep you healthy. Yes, nicotine and alcohol make you feel happy, but serotonin can also make you feel happy! Would it not make sense to choose the healthy one of the two to use like a drug? Use serotonin!

e.   Prolonged consumption of red meat, canned food, frozen food, sugar, chocolates, and junk food leads to heaviness, and a low, depressed mood. In addition, they break down a strong immune system. Do not eat more than one of these per week.

f.   If you can, avoid the medicines you take that can contribute to depression. Do not stop important medication without consulting your doctor first about an alternative medicine you can benefit from, but here are some medicines that can cause depression: Antibiotics, barbiturates, amphetamines, pain killers, ulcer drugs, anticonvulsants, beta-blockers, anti-Parkinson's drugs, birth control pills, high blood pressure drugs, heart medications and psychotropic drugs. All these medications break down the vitamins in your blood and use it to kill a specific disease, but those vitamins are also required to keep your mood up where it is supposed to be.

Here are some extra cool things to know about your new diet!

Every day the use of your body damages some of the molecules in your body… This is normal, and you call these damaged molecules "free radicals". These free radicals are the molecules that make us age faster, get sick quicker, and look a lot older than we really are. They even cause dysfunction of certain things in our body, like becoming impotent with age. Anti-oxidants take these damaged molecules out of our bodies! Eat foods high in anti-oxidants! Examples of these anti-oxidants are vitamin C, vitamin E, and beta-carotene! Your body needs a variety of vitamins, minerals, oils, amino acids, carbs, protein, and anti-oxidants every day to perform at its best!

Some of the foods that contain good anti-oxidants are apricots, broccoli, cantaloupe, carrots, peaches, pumpkin, spinach, sweet potato, blueberries, grapefruit, kiwi, oranges, peppers, potatoes, strawberries, tomato, nuts and seeds, vegetable oils, and wheat germ.

If you need to be more alert during the day (noradrenaline), if you are in constant need of motivation (dopamine), or even if you need a healthy energy booster, your body may not be getting enough tyrosine. This is an amino acid available in most protein-rich foods like tuna, turkey, or chicken! Eat healthy portions of these proteins daily! Remember to make a daily eating plan for yourself, eating six small meals a day. Cook your food with healthy oils only! This diet is very healthy for any person, but especially for depressed or anxious individuals!

Chapter 5.4

Exercise your chemical glands

Ok, now we get to the next very important aspect of fighting depression, and this is the most important thing for overcoming depression. It is to exercise! Even if you could do everything else for your depression, including a better diet, and meditation, and self-motivation, and even if you see a therapist every day and use anti-depressant medication, your psychiatrist will still tell you to exercise at home or at the gym regularly.

Depression can sometimes be so deliberating that it is very difficult to pull yourself out of that dark hole, and though exercise is the last thing on your mind, it is the actual and most important thing you need to do to immediately start feeling good, because being an active person who moves around a lot and exercises, feels great. This should be so important to you, and to everyone, that you would do anything except miss exercise. I mean if the queen is being tortured and you could do something about it, or if the sun is going to burn up and you're the only person that can fix it, you still need to put exercise above all those things.

Even if you feel so tired and worn out and negative, and you just feel so bad that you wish you could rather be in a coma than experience so much turmoil from your depression, you still need to get up, go out there, and lift some weights! That is how important it is to exercise, and that is not even the beginning, so do not get me started!

If you can gym with this in your mind every time, you will soon feel like everybody else who just cannot wait to go to the gym. Every time your mind tells you: "Why bother?" you have to get up and do it again, and again. It is not going to make a permanent difference in one week! Everyone is different, and some people have to do this for a month, two months, or even a year before they start to feel better.

You cannot miss a single session, not even if your body is so sore it feels like a burning fire. This must become more important than all your other responsibilities, I mean above all! Again, when you start to feel better you cannot quit yet! Because then you may fall back into depression ten times harder (if that is even possible). You have to continue every day, for as long as you can breathe!

I am not talking about job-related exercise; I mean real healthy cardiovascular exercise. What is cardio-exercising? These exercises include anything that gets your blood pumping and your heart rate up! It helps your lungs saturate more oxygen for your blood. These exercises include walking, jogging, running, boxing, playing cricket, lifting weights, or doing other repetitive exercise that gets you fit, and keeps you fit. What is that? Do you not know how? Learn! Ask! Research! Notice! How do you think all those other people learnt the exercise!

Why not just dare to be someone who is going places?

Now what will happen if you exercise like this? Well:

- First, you will have an increased sense of mastery, which means you will feel in control of your life.
- It gives you much more confidence, and it helps you feel great about your body.
- All the glands in your body that creates chemicals like adrenalin, and serotonin, and the others you learned about, will also exercise in creating more good chemicals.
- Your level of energy during the day will increase because of increased adrenalin production, and a healthier heart.
- The more you sweat, the more stress-chemicals leave your body, allowing you to be stress-free. However, some people cannot sweat, and they generally cry more because that too releases toxic stress chemicals. It is good to cry!
- You will also have great self-esteem.

- Exercising will distract you from your worries, and of course, it gives you the chance to take out some frustrations on a boxing bag for example.
- It improves your health and body, which lifts your mood even further. When you exercise, your brain actually grows! All those neuron-highways you learnt about will grow like crazy only when you exercise!
- It will help you sleep better, and to wake up refreshed, which is a huge problem solved for depressed people.
- You will feel awake, and calm, but powerful and energetic at the same time, because your body will practice creating good chemicals faster. This also greatly helps you to have a clear mind.

The best time for depressed people will be to exercise in the morning, because it releases energy through adrenalin and other chemicals, and helps you feel great for the whole day. Most times, it is difficult to think you have to start exercising in the next 5 minutes, and then you seriously want to avoid it.

The cool thing is though; if you can just stand up and gym for 10 minutes, you will already feel better about exercising. You just have to remember with every one of your exercising sessions, that even though you might not be feeling in the mood to gym, if you force yourself to do just those first 10 minutes, you will feel up-and-awake, the rest of the session will feel great, and after you are done you will feel amazing the whole day!

As you are getting ready for your next exercise, and you feel those negative thoughts crawl their way up to you, interrupt them. Seriously, as soon as those thoughts start, decide to stand up immediately and to say "I am going to get my water, and I am going to exercise because I will feel better, and look sexier! I can, I want to, so I will!"

Chapter 5.5

Make your exercise fun

Most times depressed people are so tired and exhausted that every little task they see, looks like a great effort. Depressed or anxious people even lose interest in all their hobbies, because they start to seem more like effort, instead of fun! They even tend to sit at home all the time, and say no to invitations from their friends! They would like to go, and want to know how their friends are doing. Yes, they really want to be there with their friends, but it is too great effort sometimes. They cannot simply snap out of something like this! It is a real problem they are facing and need support to find full freedom. This is the complete and utter truth!

How do we overcome that terrible feeling of inertia? Well, here are a few important tips:

A. One way is to keep it simple. It does not take too much exercise to lift your mood each day, but it does require you to exercise every day without skipping a day. So set simple goals for yourself in the beginning: Start by walking around the block 3 times before work, or when waking up in the morning. Then try to walk a little further every month. After this, you can go back to three laps a day, but now you can jog instead of walk. This will make it easy for you to get started. Then later you may increase the exercise a little every time, with things like some boxing if you are into it, or a game of cricket, tennis, or some push-ups! Keep on adding until you reach your full goal!

B. Also, remember to go easy on yourself. It is so easy to become critical and judgemental of yourself if you are depressed, and now is not the time to kick yourself. You might not be able to handle a lot of exercise in the beginning, so feel good about what you can do. Whether you go outside and work in the yard, or take your dog for a walk or run up and down the stairs a few times, it all counts! Just do it every day, even after you start to feel better! Never give up! You will not ever give up!

C. If you do not want to exercise every day, you can take a friend with you who is very active. The two of you can then gym hard twice a week, or do kickboxing or something else that you like. By the way, do not be afraid of physical exercise like kickboxing! You will not get hurt! Once you joined a kickboxing club for instance, they teach you everything from the beginning! You can repeat it as often as you like! No one will look at you, because everyone is too tired to think straight most times anyway, or are concentrating on becoming better! Ladies will also benefit a lot from kickboxing. When you feel ready, maybe in two months' time, you can exercise more than twice a week.

D. If you like yoga, spend a few minutes going through some simple poses. If you like fresh air, go for a good walk, or a bike ride. Besides, after you are done you will feel better. Do it every day, or even three times a day if you can! The point is, we humans need to be active, and keep our bodies moving during all the time we are awake. They we will be healthy and feel like a normal person.

E. Do you like table tennis (Ping-Pong)? What do you think about spin the bottle, or "truth-or-dare"? Do you like dancing, or singing? Maybe you would like to know how to train animals and research obedience training... I believe you could teach an animal some new tricks! Whatever it is, keep on moving during the day! Standing up is hard, but once you are up, it already feels much better!

F. If you ever seem to stop exercising because you just feel too tired again, do yourself a favour and read this part again, and again, so you remember everything again and maybe hearing the motivation, will help you do what you need to, to feel better. You somehow need to do these things time and again! Do not waste time by falling back into that dark hole every time.

You are going to need to get all the way through eventually, so do it right even if you have to fall out of bed on purpose and laugh at yourself to get going. Try it, it feels good and it is fun laughing at yourself because you did it on purpose. Then starting to walk or jog lightly will be much easier in the morning. If you are worried people at home will look at you funny, ask yourself this: "Is it any of their business"? You need to get some backbone and say this a billion times a day if you have to "I just don't care about what anyone thinks"! "It is my life! I will do whatever it is I want to do, because I am a person too, and I have the right to do this too"!

G. Make your exercise a social thing. Try to find a friend to talk with while the both of you are walking around the block, or walking to the shop, and if you do not have any, GET SOME! Start talking to people and make new friends if you do not have a friend that can exercise with you. Talking to people can raise your energy and remind you that you are not alone. Any friend will do! While you walk, force yourself to have a skip in your step. Make yourself feel like you have rhythm.

   Whenever you take a walk somewhere, always expect something great to happen, even if nothing happened. You might just get lucky! Do not worry, you do not have to move like a maniac if you start with a rhythm, just walk comfortably with an upbeat heart and maybe a good song to whistle. Really, make mountains of good friends, and stop thinking about that nagging problem! Really, will the world end if you decide to forget about all your problems for just 10 minutes and relax? Talk to people. It is not hard at all, and everybody does it. The conversation always starts with "Hi there, my name is John. It's nice to meet you..."

H. Also, try to go outside for your exercises sometimes, because even a little sunshine can help boost your mind and remind you that there is a world out there. You can participate in as much as you can handle. Do not push yourself too hard for the first few months, because exercise must be something you enjoy. Otherwise, you will not feel motivated to keep on doing it. You will feel fit, energetic, and more confident sooner than you think! You can also ask a doctor for some exercising tips that you might find fun and interesting. Remember that some exercise is better than none is! Do something every day!

Chapter 5.6

Reasons to exercise

Exercise helps for so many things, like high blood pressure, diabetes, arthritis, depression, anxiety, sex-drive, skin-tone, studying, and general health. Studies have proven that the physical and psychological benefits of regular exercise can improve mood, and reduce anxiety more than anything else can, including medicine.

The reason you feel so great after exercising, is because exercising increases oxygen in your bloodstream, and stretches your body while getting your heart rate a little higher, and this makes it easy for the body to release the "feel-good chemicals" like lovable endorphins or excitable dopamine, or happy adrenalin, and many other things, into your bloodstream. At the same time, you sweat out all the toxic chemicals that harm your body and mind! Some chemicals help your body make even more of themselves, and help your body create more serotonin, causing you to heal permanently from depression if you can just hold it up long enough.

Remember, exercising yourself to near-death is not the answer! You want to stay motivated not to skip a single day, and light exercise is perfect for a while. So is hard exercise twice a week for two months, until you feel generally better and ready to make your exercise program more intense, without feeling afraid that you will stop exercising lovable endorphins or excitable dopamine, smart serotonin, or happy adrenalin, into your bloodstream. Work slowly, step-by-step, until you are ready for the next step with every step!

Exercising is actually so great, because it balances your body not to feel too busy, or too calm. In other words, it can bring you out of depression into happiness, and it can bring people who have anxiety to a relaxed state, and allow both those people to heal permanently from their anxiety or depression, and to feel great in the process.

How does exercise help depression and anxiety? Well, other than releasing the feel-good chemicals that cause depression to heal, it also kills the chemicals in the immune system that can worsen depression, exercise also increases body temperature, and this has calming effects. It is healthy because it helps your body metabolise the vitamins, minerals, and oils in your body to something useful in keeping you healthy and symptom-free from things like diabetes, and many other things.

If you gym regularly, your body will release its feel-good chemicals and you'll be fit and your body will feel pumped, keeping your body warmer and calmer and much stronger for the whole day and not just in the time you exercise. It will make you a confident person. If you gym, you will sweat, and remember that this is your body releasing the stress-chemicals out of your body, but sweating in a warm bath is not the same. Exercise is the only way to sweat and release stress-chemicals. Do the research if you do not believe this!

Never forget that exercise builds confidence, because you start to meet your exercise goals and challenges, and soon you also feel a lot better about your appearance, and soon exercise will even teach you how to say no, or how to show people calmly that they may not walk all over you and get by with it. It takes your mind off worries, allowing your brain to restructure itself to a healthy state while you take out your frustrations and while you are distracted from your problems your brain is stimulated in other areas that were very quiet while you were in your depressed state.

It enables you to have positive social interaction. Even just smiling when you walk past someone outside, will make those good chemicals oose through your body. Exercise allows you to cope in a healthy way, as happy people do it. Trying to feel better by drinking alcohol, or dwelling your mind on how badly you feel, or just hoping your depression or anxiety will go away on its own can only lead to your symptoms becoming worse.

It is a good idea to try to do what you usually enjoy. When you are depressed, it is hard to enjoy anything, but think about what you would normally like to do when you are not depressed. You may not enjoy it in the moment, but if you keep at it for longer than a few minutes, it will start to feel better, and even a small change in your mood can make a big difference.

Any exercise that gets your heart pumping is best for permanently overcoming depression and anxiety. Things like running, lifting weights, playing basketball, swimming, or doing any other fitness activities are great, but so can gardening, washing your car, strolling around the block and other less-intense activities to start with. Anything that gets you off the couch and moving is exercise that will improve your mood.

Try to exercise for 15 minutes at a time, three times a day, or you can do a proper workout in the morning, but spreading your exercises throughout your day is a very good idea for a depressed person. Consider cycling to work if you live close enough or parking a little further away from the shop's entrance, or take the stairs instead of the elevator, to get moving more and exercise your body into making those good chemicals.

Get some posters with motivation on that you can put up in your house, so you can look at them whenever you do not want to exercise. Make some posters that remind you of the good things exercise does to us!

Never stop thinking outside the box! Now by this time I have a feeling that you might already have about a billion excuses as to not being able to do the things you learnt so far… Well, let us look at a practical example about this before we continue to learn.

There is a woman, called Lucy. She is twenty-nine years old, has three kids of ages two, five, and six. Her husband left her, and now she has to maintain two different jobs in order for her to keep her kids in school, and herself in a warm bed. She works from six in the morning, to four in the afternoon as a receptionist, and then from eight at night until eleven o'clock at night, as an emergency consultant for a bank. She does not have friends because she has decided that all people are the same… She also does not like herself because she acts funny and she is not as beautiful as she wants to be, and her parents told her she is worth absolutely nothing. She developed depression. Lucy does not have a medical aid or the money she needs to see a therapist at all. How will someone like this get out of depression?

What do you think? What advice would you have given Lucy if she asked you? Did you learn anything from this book so far? What is the first step?

Admit you have a problem. Find out what exactly is the problem you are facing, Lucy. Wake up in the morning thirty minutes earlier, with a smile on your face! Stand up immediately and interrupt your thoughts to expect something good that will happen to you today, and get enough food ready for yourself that you could have six meals every day. Start with eggs in the morning on wheat bread toast, an apple at teatime with some juice, that leftover chicken-noodles from last night as your lunch, then a handful of nuts at around three-o'clock with a cup of herbal tea. Just before leaving your first job, eat a slice of banana bread. Remember that this is just an example Lucy, and you can eat whatever you like.

Park as far from the entrance of your job as possible so you can get some air on your way in. Be proud of your work, and do not offer help to people if you do not intend to help! You are entitled to rest sometimes too! After work, pick up your kids from the day-care centre, and go home. Turn on some music, and turn into a woman who says, "I can do anything I set my mind to!" Get the stove on and make dinner. It only has to take an hour at most. Do you disagree? Well, what about the time you had to cook for someone and started late? Did that go well? Could it have? There is your answer! Stop moaning, get rhythm in your hips after that long day at work, and cook to the sound of that positive music! While you are waiting for the food, drink some water again, go to the toilet, and take a stretch or two.

Take some time to relax and just have a chat with your kids, show some interest in their homework without helping them with answers, and then get your uniform on for your second job. Do not forget that book you wanted to take with you! Remember that now the weekend is already one day closer! Give your list of duties to your nanny; take a late-night snack with you like a smoothie, or a sandwich, and head on to the shop to buy your groceries. Get it in the car, and head on to your second job.

Stop window-shopping on your way so that you can resign from this second job after you paid your debt in full. Come home from work, do a little yoga, take a nice comforting warm bath, and jump into bed.

In your free time, look for a higher-paying job, and stay positive! Call people and ask them how their day is going! Stop gossiping with your co-workers at work, and start to realise that your job is a professional place. Smile at people; ask someone to help you with some things that you will not have time for at work, and just say no to people asking you for help with things that you cannot fit into your schedule! Do not ever try to make people happy! Find a way! You will learn how to say no and feel good later in the book!

You really do not have an excuse! Lucy just found an answer. Yes, it may still sound a little too busy, but she is still doing it! She is going to do this until she really starts to feel better! Then her mind will be clearer, and her body will feel relaxed in the midst of her busy day! She will now have the power to talk to people, and to start looking for a better solution, like a hubby, or a single better-paying job!

You may say, "She cannot even exercise"! Yes, she can! She can run up and down the stairs at home for three laps before ever going into her house, or she can do some running around the block in lunchtime at work. Can you believe that she will actually feel great at work if she does this? Lucy can even dance at home with herself while she is cooking. Then she can have a laugh at funny movements because she just does not care!

The point is she does the best with what she has at that moment. If she can only sleep five hours, at least she is not watching television until three in the morning! She is actually sleeping!

At work, she interrupts her thoughts and continually motivates herself! While she is at home, she decides to forget about her problems at work, because she cannot do anything about them from home any way!

Lucy will not have to do this forever… She is going to make some even more drastic changes in her life shortly after this. She is not sitting down, feeling sorry for herself. She does not allow people to walk all over her, because she decided to get real with those who are mean to her. Lucy does her work, and leaves her job proud at night, not walking over other people either.

She asks for help, she gets the right food in every day, and she looks forward to the weekend so she can play cricket with her kids, have a well-deserved picnic with them, or go swimming with them. She actually tries to be part of her kids' lives, and motivates them to be outside more often rather than sitting in front of the television the whole time, because she knows that sitting and sitting every day will cause her kids to have the same depression she has to fight now!

She does not feel as depressed as before now! At first, she felt heartbroken because no one likes her, everyone tries to use her, she is alone, and she makes mistakes, and feels worthless. Now though, she decided to get some backbone! She went out there, made some friends, decided she is not going to stop until she is happy, and she is not going to give up, even if she has to start over again a thousand times!

Do you get my drift here? Stop your excuses now! Yes, Lucy still gets bad days, and she still gets tired sometimes! The point is that she is not going to give up! She does not need people to make her happy, because she already decided she is going to be happy. On those days where she comes off work early, she can go and have a milkshake completely on her own and enjoy it! She can even go for a walk and just enjoy the scenery without rushing for anything. Once she found a way to see a therapist, she is going to go, until she can start on a new fresh page!

Lucy can definitely be independent, and have a happy home of her own, with less stress, and more fun. She can definitely have all the things she wants, like a beautiful home, and smart children who are good, and she can have that black Labrador named Lucky, with friends that do not walk over her! Lucy is going to get lucky, right after she made her decision that she is going to do whatever it takes, no matter how she feels right now. She will make the change happen, until her circumstances change, and her happiness happens! Her kids will love her, and she will allow them to bring friends home sometimes and get dirty. Lucy will not clean up after them, but rather discipline them while never breaking them down, until everyone is happy.

Lucy is going to change her life, because only she can!

Read on warrior!

Chapter 5.7

Sleeping the right way

You should also get enough sleep, BUT NOT TOO MUCH! This is a big problem for people who suffer from depression!

You have to make sure beyond anything else that you only sleep as much as you should in every 24-hour cycle. If you are between 5-10 years old, you need 10-11 hours of sleep every night, if you are 10-17 years old, you will need 8.5-9.5 hours of sleep, and if you are an adult from 18 years or older, you need 7-9 hours of sleep. People who are above 40 years of age need less sleep, and this is roughly 6-7 hours of sleep in every 24-hour cycle. Even if a healthy person feels tired during the day, it may be due to many late nights of work, but another reason is too much sleep.

If you sleep too much, even if you are awake in bed, your body creates too much melatonin for your body. This chemical should only be present while you are sleeping. Excess melatonin makes you tired during the time you need to be awake. So yes, there is even concrete scientific evidence that too much sleep will keep you tired during the day.

One of the reasons why a depressed person does not sleep well at night is because of the fact that depression causes your biological clock to go crazy and to function incorrectly.

Sleeping and waking up at the right times, using anti-depressants, and exercising will help your biological clock to realign itself, but you have to use it until your depression is completely gone before you can sleep like a baby at night. While you are on the medication, if you plan your sleeping habits carefully, and stick to the program until your body will automatically use those habits, like in a healthy person, you will enjoy your sleep at night and feel great the next morning.

What are the things you need to do for better sleep at night?

- Well, you have to exercise every day, and try to stay physically active the whole time until you start relaxing for bed. You can do anything from playing Monopoly, to chatting with friends, or using the computer, playing video games, singing to yourself in the bathroom, or even dancing while you are cleaning your house... Whatever you can keep yourself busy with, but do not ever sit still for too long during the day, doing nothing. Go out with friends, go see a movie, or chat, take a swim, or do something else you enjoy.

- If you eat a big meal at night, make sure you finish eating at least 2 hours before bedtime, but one hour should be fine if you eat six small dishes every day.

- Also, avoid caffeine, alcohol, nicotine and any other drugs or depressant products close to bedtime.

- You need to create a sleep-conducive environment that is completely dark, quiet, comfortable, and cool. Sleeping without this tip is not healthy, and this is the reason why getting out of bed is so difficult for some people. If you are not used to it, GET used to it! It is healthier! Your brain needs to do what it wants to do at night, and not be distracted with sounds or flashing lights while you are asleep. This will allow your brain to repair itself for effectively handling the next day's stress.

  If you sleep with the television or radio on, you are increasing your chance of getting a heart attack, high cholesterol, or even diabetes or some other problem somewhere in your life! Do I really need to explain this too? It is not healthy! Talk to your doctor about this.

- Make sure you sleep on a comfortable mattress and pillows, and try to make most of your sleep time on your back, as this is the healthiest position for your heart. Sleeping on your sides or chest can be uncomfortable for your lungs and heart, keeping your brain busy stressing. Make sure you are comfortable. It is ok if you turn onto your sides as you sleep. Part of sleeping comfortably also includes going to the toilet before bed, and drinking enough water before bed that you do not become thirsty during bedtime.

- Then you can create a regular relaxing bedtime routine such as soaking in a hot bath, listening to soothing music, doing yoga, praying for someone or reading, meditation on positive thoughts, or even a nice comforting massage, but you should begin with this at least an hour before you go to bed. Do this every night. If you skip a day, you have to start all over again, losing the progress you made with your biological clock. This must become a habit for all of us, but especially for depressed people, for it to become natural and an every-day thing! Do not watch TV right before bedtime. You have to relax your body and mind away from concentrating, an hour before bedtime.

- The most important thing here is you need to go to bed and get out of bed at the exact same time every day of the week, including weekends. This will realign your biological clock, and soon you will be amazed to see that you will automatically wake up at the same time every day, feeling refreshed and ready to get out of bed, even without an alarm. It will not happen straight away, but you need to do it every night until it does.

  A good idea would be to try going to bed by 10, and to set your alarm to wake up at seven. This will give younger depressed people 9 hours of sleep, but you can make a plan that suits you and your working schedule perfectly, so you get the sleep you need in every 24 hours, without sleeping for more than the recommended hours in every age group. These things will all help to realign your biological clock, really keeping you awake when you need to be.

- When you wake up in the morning, do not lay in bed for longer than 5 minutes. You can wake up, take a few deep breaths, take a long confortable stretch or three, and jump out of bed like a crazy person. Fall out of bed if you want to, or crawl even. You can do whatever you want! This will jolt your body and brain to the wake state, helping you feel good during the day because of a burst of healthy adrenalin shooting through your blood. Do not think you cannot have fun while you are getting out of bed, because it can be amazing! Just remember to expect great things to happen in your day just before getting out of bed. Fall out of bed on purpose, if you know you will not get hurt, and then just lay there laughing at yourself as loudly as you want to! See yourself having a good day as you see the sun shine through the curtains. Who says you cannot? Just learn to have some fun and laugh!

- This next tip is the second-most important one for sleeping deeply at night, and making you fall asleep quicker than usual. Use your bedroom only for sleep and sex! You have to keep "sleep stealers" out of the bedroom completely, because if you do not, your sub-conscious mind will see the computer or the TV close to your bed and it will start to link the bed with the computer. Meaning your brain will try to stay awake in bed, like you would stay awake in front of your computer. This will happen even if you only see the computer or TV in your room, without using it. If you can take it out so you do not even have to see them in the bedroom, it is even better!

These sleep-stealers are watching TV while lying in bed, using a computer or reading in bed. These are terribly unhealthy for depressed and even healthy people. During the time you are awake, it is very important to keep your body upright and active. Sitting is fine, but lying on the couch is not! After the activities of the day are over, and you have eaten your last meal at least an hour before bed, you can immediately start doing something relaxing.

You can do anything you learnt earlier, except watching TV or playing video games though! Try to do these relaxing exercises outside the room. The point is to take the last hour of the day to relax your brain, not to concentrate! Then you can go to bed, turn off the light immediately, and start sleeping immediately. If you are a Christian, you can pray and read your Bible outside and away from your bed, and this will be great for relaxing before bedtime. However, make sure by the time you go to bed, it will allow the whole amount of sleep time you need at your age. TV, radio, reading, cell phones, and computers, and anything else that you use while you are awake should be outside the bedroom, even if you do not intend to use them. Stay upright and active during your wake time, and relax outside your room before bedtime!

All these things will be sure to make you sleep deeper and more comfortably at night, and it will take away most of the tossing-and-turning before sleep, and it will allow you to feel really awake and full of energy during the day.

Chapter 5.8

Tips for a better day

Here are some other things you may do every day for you to start feeling better, but it is very important to use medicine and therapy to get permanent and maximum results for your mood if you have any form of depression that is higher than mild-depression: And do not stress, we are getting close to the end now...

* Get lots of sunshine. The sun enables your body to create vitamins, specifically vitamin D, which is very healthy for your body and skin. Take a quick 10-minute daily tan, or do something in the sun, but try not to burn though.

* A very important thing you should not ever do is listen to any sad, slow, irritating, or depressing music, EVER! Delete it all off your phone. Do not even accidentally browse past it, and do not listen to any music that "speaks" to you too often. If you like to sometimes listen to intense music that has a deep message, it is ok to hear, one in every 100 or so that you listen to, but do not make it a habit. Only listen to constant happy music that is upbeat and makes you want to party! The only time you should listen to relaxing music is if you have an anxiety-related depression that causes you to become restless and stressing, or just before you go to bed, but it should still be positive relaxing music. Never listen to bad music, even when you are feeling bad. Music that reminds you of a negative past is also a very bad idea,

no matter what your excuse! The same thing goes for reading, and watching movies.

The point is you want to feel better when you are feeling blue, and negative music will not help you one bit! Do you think happy people do this? If you listen to music when you are in the car, or at the office, or in the workshop, a very effective thing you can do is to have a slight beat in your body while you are listening. Just move your hips, your shoulders, or even your neck and head constantly while you listen. You can even hum, or whistle the song to yourself. Not only will it keep your muscles loose and comfortable, it will also cause them to not ever make you feel tensed, which in turn will make your day more effective, and even the slightest movement will make your body release those feel-good chemicals a lot easier.

- Experience laughter, this is physically good medicine for depression, and for a healthier body and mind. You have seen earlier that good chemicals will even make you recover from flu or a heart attack quicker than usual. So how do you make these chemicals, other than with the things you learned so far? Well, you can laugh. Did you know laughter is also free? Make a funny face and laugh at yourself, listen to jokes, or make jokes with people! Watch comedies on TV, watch cartoons like SpongeBob, dance like a crazy person when you are alone, or you can even dance badly on purpose in front of others with a smile on your face, and laugh with your friends at your joke, or even laugh for no reason if you have to. I think I will probably still watch SpongeBob and do all these other fun things after I am 90! Laughter enables your body to create adrenalin, endorphins, and some dopamine along with some other cool chemicals, and most of these chemicals are the neurotransmitters your brain needs to heal, and to enhance your mood.
- Talk to people, or even talk aloud about the things you are thinking about when you are alone. This will definitely get you in the mood to get up and do something about it.
- If you have many plans, write them down on a checklist. It makes you feel more in control of a busy life.
- Read books and do research on the internet about depression. It helps to know everything there is to know about what you are up against

here. Though this book covers almost everything there is to know about depression and anxiety, it is not the only piece of information available out there about this topic.

- Happy people are also not always the most gracious people! Do you want to know why? Well, because they have learned how to say NO! You cannot do everything for everyone all the time and be a happy person. YOU have to decide, would you rather work yourself to death, or would you be happy. Learn to say no, and practice to say no whenever someone is expecting something from you in a time when you want to do something you enjoy. Be diligent in saying no when you need some time for yourself. Have place for others, but say no sometimes. You are a person too!

   Get into the habit of doing the same thing as these people. Ask for help, and ask for favours now and then, even if you can do many things on your own, ask for help anyway. Allow others to do some things for you anyway, because you need to have rest or time to have fun as these people do! That is why others lean on each other; it is because they know everybody is responsible for their own joy.

   You do not have to care if something is not going to be perfect if you leave it in someone else's hands. Will it matter a hundred years from now? Do you think it will matter one week from now? No, it will not! No one cares! If you struggle to say no, here is some help: If someone asks you to do something for them but you have plans to do something you enjoy, then just say: "Sorry, I'm going to be a little busy later, but why don't you try THIS to fix your problem? It might make that thing get solved quickly." Read that sentence again. Give those people a recommendation to make the task go easier for them, because it will show them that you still care about them, even though you cannot help at that time. You can still help people, but do not get your joy stolen by helping everybody all the time!

- Did you know that crying also relieves depression? The proteins found in emotional tears are hormones that build up to very high levels when the body withstands emotional stress. If these stress-chemicals did not discharge at all, they would build up to toxic levels that weaken the immune system, and other biological processes. If you do not cry every time you feel like it, you are making yourself sick! Crying is good, and it takes a strong man to cry, not a weak one. Let people say what they want to. For women this may be a little easier. So cry when you feel like it, even if you have to step away from the crowd to do it, but crying will relieve your built-up emotional depressed state for a while, every time you cry. Holding in the tears is not healthy.

- It is also a good idea to get a close pet to care for, but a pet is there to pet, not just to feed. Am I making sense here?

- Another amazing way to fight depression is by singing. If you do not know any good songs, go and find yourself some positive songs you can listen to every day. Learn the words, and whenever you feel blue, you can sing it wherever you are. This stimulates dopamine production in your body (if you like the song), and keeps your mind off your troubles. I have a song that is not even English, but I copied the lyrics off the internet, and took two days to learn it, because I really enjoy singing it. He Mele No Lilo is the name, and it is the theme song from Lilo and Stitch. You can sing in the shower, at home, or outside. If you want, you can even whistle a good positive song you know. If you cannot sing well, sing anyway, and then have a laugh about yourself as you sing. Just relax! You do not have to be so hard on yourself about everything!

- You may also need to move away from the things that cause you to feel depressed constantly, because some of those things can pull you back into that dark black hole so quickly, that you struggle to get out every time. Things like sitting still for too long, or lying in bed awake for too long, being around negative friends and people too often, or being around things that remind you of stressful events or work all the time. Get rid of those things, be around positive people, move a little further away than quick driving distance from negative people if you have to, and use your hobbies as distractions.

    If life forces you to be around negative people during the day, you can distract yourself with earphones and music, or simply do not listen to their talking. Maybe you can motivate them to be positive while you talk to them. Do it every single time you possibly can.

- Another thing you can do to start feeling better is to just go outside sometimes for a few minutes, and to notice the fresh air touching your skin, the sunlight giving you that warm cosy feeling, the nature all around you, like the birds chirping, or even the cracking sounds a tree will make if there is wind. Feel the grass between your toes, or the water flowing over your hands as you wash them. You can even listen to the sounds of the city but go outside and just take a moment to take in your environment. Do not think about anything else! Just take five minutes to relax. The world is still going to exist after those five minutes! This will feel so great every time you do it, especially when you just get outside and that warm, comforting, fresh feeling melts your worries away. It really helps to put things in perspective. There are more wonderful things out there than problems, resentment, and stress!

- You can even get into the habit of taking notice of some things you do not normally notice, like walking barefoot outside. Just let your toes feel the crisp and fresh cold blades of grass pushing through them as you walk or stand outside, or the feeling of the earth while you walk on the sand. Sometimes we forget how refreshing water flows over our hands as we wash them, because we are always stressing too much.

  Yes, all these tasks also stimulates those chemical glands in your body to inject more good chemicals into your blood, and just do it often enough, and those glands would have had some exercise. Therefore, they will be bigger, and they will keep on creating more of those good chemicals for you than usual. Before you know it, all those glands in your body will have little six-packs and rock-hard biceps, pumping out those chemicals in your blood like crazy! But exercising them means you are going to have to force yourself to feel good, and I don't mean just thinking you feel ok, I mean by really keeping yourself feeling very happy and excited!

- You should also try not to get depressed because you are depressed. Every time your mind tells you to feel bad because you have depression, you must interrupt that thought with a positive thought and forget about it completely. You can actually interrupt all your negative thoughts by just shaking your head, jumping up from your seat if you have to and then saying to yourself: "This is not true. I'm going to think about something positive, and something to look forward to." Think about what you are going to do this weekend, or in your free time. Try to make up a joke that you can send to someone.

Depression is an illness, and you will recover, so be positive about it! You are going to learn something not everyone knows, and you are becoming stronger than most people are, and may someday even start helping weak people become happy like you! Therefore, it is ok to go through depression, as long as you keep on walking toward recovery!

- Always try to do things differently every day. Choose three different routes to work, and drive a different one every day. If you get up in the morning, change the order in which you get things done. Maybe you get up, put on your clothes, brush your teeth, and then drink some coffee. Change it every day, sometimes you can brush your teeth first, and then drink your coffee, and then put on your clothes, but make all your daily routines interesting by changing their order every day.

  This will allow you to concentrate a little more on what you're busy doing because now you don't just follow the same structure every day without thinking anymore, and it occupies your mind and distracts it from the reason why you are depressed. Just forget those things for a while every day, it will really help. If you like three different hairstyles, wear a new one every day. Be that interesting person you really are!

- Always keep yourself busy during the day with your hobbies and interests, even if you have lost interest in them long ago. Keeping yourself busy with things will occupy your mind and keep it away from negative thoughts. Just forget negative thoughts altogether while you are fighting your depression. It is difficult, yes, but possible. A therapist can teach you some interesting tips on this too! This will exercise the good glands in your body to make good chemicals. You will know you are doing it right if you distract yourself so well, and forget about negative thoughts on purpose, that you physically feel happier.

- When you feel blue though, it is a good idea to motivate yourself, even when you are at work. You can just go to the bathroom, rinse your face in nice cold water, take a deep breath, hold your chin up slightly, with a nice and comfortable straight back, and say, "Yeah, I'm feeling confident, and I can do anything I set my mind to. I am awake, I look good, I am going to look even sexier after a year's exercise, and I am going to go through my day as an energized person. I know my potential, and I am ready for anything. If anyone bothers me, I will tell those people what I think of them in a nice way, and feel good about it. I am proud of myself. I'm getting better every day!"

- If you are a Christian, then you should know that even the Bible says you should feel good about yourself, because if you cannot love yourself, how will you love others. God wants you to feel good, and to have a great life. He wants you to have enough money. He just does not want you to become an ungenerous person when He gives you those loads of money!

- Motivation is a very interesting thing, because you can even get into the habit of motivating and complimenting other people and it would make you feel better. If you are a Christian, you can pray for your loved ones often, because it will keep your mind off your own problems. Pray for yourself too sometimes though!

- Taking regular breaks or holidays are also a good idea for overcoming depression. Go away on weekends, visit friends, or take some time off to go on a much-needed vacation with someone. Just go and relax, and think about absolutely nothing.

Forget everything, because remember: You cannot do anything about the things that stress you out at home if you are away on holiday anyway. You can think about solving them when you get back, but until then, just go have fun and forget your problems. Go out and try new things, meet new people, do new things. You need time to relax, and to forget your problems, even if it is just for a few hours now and then, or a few days every third month or so.

This will help you be more creative at solving that problem when you get back to it later. There is no point in taking a stress-relieving break or going on a distracting holiday if you take your stress with you. So while you are there, just forget completely about your depression and go out, have fun, and act as if your life is perfect. Be ecstatic, take deep breaths, and really enjoy your time.

- In addition, many times we can expect too much out of ourselves. You have to relax the constraints and expectations you put on yourself. Everyone else does this, and that is why those people are happy. A perfectionist is not a happy person. They might only seem happy, but they would experience great happiness if they just relax about things now and then.

As you have seen earlier, you do not have to live like a slob, but you also do not have to have everything perfect the whole time. Whether it is your room, or how you talk, or how you eat your food, or whatever. Just have fun. This is part of any purpose in life. Happy people know they can be miserable while trying so hard to do just everything the whole time, but they choose not to.

Lower your standards on yourself a little. Ask people to help you with big tasks. Do not try to do everything yourself. Yes, maybe everything will not be done perfectly the way you would have done it, but it will still be done and be over with, and you will not feel exhausted. Is this not the big point? If you see someone doing something wrong, you do not always have to put your nose in his or her business either! Let people make mistakes! Sometimes that is the only way we learn.

The only thing more important than having everything perfect is having joy! Can you imagine how great it must feel if you just did not care if things are not perfect, and straight, and one hundred percent right, or to just have a go-with-the-flow and enjoy it attitude? It calms you down quite a bit. The meaning of life is to enjoy it, and if you are not enjoying yours, you are wasting your life and it is all because you stress too much about things you can just forget about, and you can feel happy about not caring, as everyone does.

Do you think other people care if the curtains are dirty, or if they forget to put a full stop after a sentence? Who cares if you do not take only one point seven seconds to change gears? Do you think people care if there is dust on your TV screen? NO, they do not! That is what makes them so calm, and so happy! You have the right to enjoy life, so just live your life happy! No one is going to kill you if you decide to be a little less hard on yourself, because that is what makes everyone else feel glad inside.

Who cares if your car missed a washing day, or if you did not read 20 pages of your book today? It is only YOU! If you have something better to do sometimes, go do it!

- Relaxing is also very important for the human body. You should really start to give yourself a break more often! Stop worrying about things so much! You really do not have to. Here is a reminder for you to think on once more. If your work gets behind at the office, and you get home, does it really help stressing about it? Does your stressing at home really get the work done at the office? NO! It does not! All it does is it sends dangerous chemicals into your body that kills you a lot sooner, and stressing at home also gives you a restless night in bed, causing you to be so tired the next day at work that you get less done and make more time-consuming mistakes!

However, if you get home while you know your work is behind at the office, you can decide to drop it completely, and get a skip in your walk, with a smile and a deep breath when you enter the door. You can think about how hungry you are and about how good you are going to feel when you take off your shoes, and shower, and eat a great dinner. You can completely forget about the trouble at work, even throwing it out where it hides in the back of your mind.

If you really want to, and you are serious enough, you can find a way to do it, even if you have a job with a company cell phone! There really is no excuse for any of those people. Now, because you decided not to stress about something that you could not fix at home, you can really relax, have a good time with the production of more positive chemicals in your body, and you can really sleep sound at night.

Then when you wake up, you can feel happy and energized, and ready for the challenges of the day. Do not even think about work when you are at home or in bed, because you cannot do anything about it when you sleep. Get your rest! Then you can go to work with a brain that has rested and get a lot more work done! Does that not make perfect sense? If you have to take work home with you every day, then get it done as soon as possible so you can forget about it later and have fun before bed!

- Parents, here is a message for you too: Depression may also develop in a child if you do not make a hard effort to raise them the right way. Just because you had a bad experience with a friend in your past and do not like taking risks, does not make it fair for your kids not to have a life! People are there to lean on, we all need it, and if you decide to be depressed because you have a trust problem, it does not make it fair towards your kids.

They will become soft and brittle if you do not allow them to have friends. It is very important for you as a parent to spend a lot of time with your children from their youngest age to the end of their teenage years, and to motivate them to try billions of new things also. Children need to experience an endless amount of different things every day, like getting dirty, spending all their awake time with someone they like, playing games, fiddling with insects, learning new things, a huge amount of exercising, being confident in front of people when talking or dancing, or doing something. They have to be with an enormous amount of different people, and have the chance to experience the actions of different friends so they can cope with everything when they get older.

Do not force them to just sit around with older people and do nothing! Let them have sleepovers, even at the age of 10. They have to go through fights, and rejection sometimes, and learn how to stand up for themselves, and learn how to make many new friends. They have to eat a balanced diet, and they have to be able to go out with friends a lot even if they are five years old, or fifteen.

This will teach them that they do not have to give up on themselves if a friend decides to leave them. Saying this to your kids, and letting them learn it on their own, has a very big difference. They have to experience it for themselves. They will also learn to get a life of their own, and learn how to care about people, and they will learn facial expressions, and gestures, and many other things that develop a person into an amazing person. I am seriously not kidding with this.

Man, you do not know the beginning of what depression can really do, and I can guarantee you that isolating your child from the world will induce it in them. You have to expose your children to everything from singing, to boxing, to going out on vacation with you and bringing a friend along, and you have to let them decide what they like and what not, and not force them to do anything they don't enjoy. I am talking about hobbies here. Things like homework, cleaning their rooms, going to sleep and waking up are things they have to do. You have to be there to discipline them, without ever breaking down their confidence! You can request more information at my e-mail address!

Do not ever allow them to have hours in front of the TV, or sitting still with their cell phones, especially if they are anywhere from five to fifteen years old. You have to motivate them, always, and compliment them so they feel secure about themselves, and you seriously should not circumcise a boy EVER! Find out how to make a foreskin work before your son is born, and make it work, and leave your son's property alone!

Invite your kids to have fun with you outside the house, and do it every day! Failing in even one of these things may cause major depression and long-term depression in a child that forces them to become something they do not want to be, and it causes an unnecessary effort for them to become happy again, years of struggle.

Isolating them from the world and only allowing them to sit in front of the TV when they are five, or only forcing them to study without also having fun, will cause their chemical glands in their bodies not to develop. Allow and motivate them to date in school, and to play rugby, or hockey, or to do anything good they want to try out.

Also, if you do not have anything good to say, then rather do not say anything at all to your kids. I do not mean that you should not reprimand them when they disobey you. On the contrary, you must display an image of "no nonsense". If you ask them to take a bath, and they disobey, they have to receive punishment, whether it is corporate or conventional! Do not repeat a command three times, but also do not give them too many unnecessary commands. This is a much more serious thing than you can ever imagine.

Of course you have to protect them, and give them good advice about bad things, but you have to introduce everything to them in life that they might enjoy, and motivate them to continue. Compliments are also very important for a child. Do this from the time they say their first word, to the time they are at least 18, without stopping even once. Then your relationship with your kids will be a lot greater.

Children need to be extremely active and motivated when they are young, and they should have at least 98% of happy and good feelings in the house while they grow up. Children will make mistakes, and laughing at them, or rejecting them about these things will cause something you will never be able to bear. You have to set an active and good example in front of your kids, and not fight so they can hear you! You can still punish them if they continue to do bad things after you had a talk about it, but screaming at them, or judging them is the worst thing you can do.

Your job and your past is not an excuse for killing the dreams of your children! Were YOU not the one who made the choice to have children? Well, then you had better be ready to raise them with a smile, and with effort and care. If you cause them to have depression by neglecting your responsibility to teach them, it is YOUR fault then that they are still living in your house ten years after they came out of school! It is not their fault! You cannot punish them for how you raised them! Do you agree?

You, parents, are the ones that show your kids everything for the first time! They will never forget that first time you showed them something about life, and they will believe all you show them is the right way of doing things. If you think it is too late, it is not. Just help them get over their depression if they developed it, and you have to make an effort to know if they do in fact have depression, because it is not something they will just tell you. Make an effort.

- One last important thing is to try to let go of things people did to you in the past that disappointed you. Because poisoning yourself with something that is in the past is not worth anything, and you are wasting your time being you! Get over it! Those people in your past who hurt you are not crying right now, they forgot about it long ago and are having fun. Is it worth letting them win by feeling bad all the time? NO! Show yourself that you are better because you got over that little thing and you live a happy life with all the things you like!

- Think about forgiveness… What is forgiveness? Why should I forgive? Who deserves forgiveness? Did you know that forgiveness actually has absolutely nothing to do with the other person? The purpose of forgiving someone is not to make those other people happy! God says in the Christian Bible, that forgiveness is essential for life. You have to forgive people who hurt you, so that 'you' will survive! God teaches this in the Bible! Only when you forgive, will your body stop killing you! How is this possible? Well, whenever you do not forgive, your body creates toxins that break down your body's health and mind.

- Oh yes, and remember to take a bath and brush your teeth every day! This is very important! You may not know this, but your body is infected with viruses and sickness every day! It is in the very air you breathe! There is no way to avoid it. There is a very strong fight in your body every day, and every night to kill these diseases and sickness. If you do not bath once a day, your body becomes overwhelmed with these viruses, and that can tire a person quite a bit! Part of exercising, and eating the right healthy foods to stay healthy, is taking care of your general hygiene. Do not take this to an extreme by never getting dirty though! This is not healthy either! Your immune system will not ever learn how to fight illness if you live in a bubble. Get dirty, but take a bath once a day.

- One last cool thing in this chapter: If you feel a tickle or an itch on your body, NEVER scratch it! An itch on your body means your body is repairing your skin in that area. If you are strong enough not to scratch an itch also does two other things. It gives you the confidence of a lion, because it is such a hard thing to accomplish, and having an occasional itch or tickle releases dopamine and serotonin in your body, while at the same time eliminating toxins. Leave that itch until it goes away on its own, enjoy it when you are being tickled, and do not forget to tickle back!

Chapter 5.9

"Best Friend" Syndrome

If a best friend decides to leave you, or if your best friend is misusing you to the point where you feel so uncomfortable, and even talking to them about it does not help and you know you have to end the friendship with them... Does it solve anything when you spend days, and weeks, and even months thinking about it? Does it really make anything better if you just sit there in a bad mood, upset, and grumpy for hours at a time? Do you really feel great when you go to bed at night and toss-and-turn and cry, get mad, and sit with this terrible conflict in your heart?

NO! It does not do you one bit of good! I bet you that friend will not do it either! You have to decide to GET OVER IT! Really, just get over it. Is it really a great friend if they treat you as if you are a piece of garbage just good enough when they need something? Sometimes bad friends have such a big power over us, because we really like those people sometimes... But all it is, is those people had so much time practicing how to manipulate people into getting what they want, that they blind our eyes. Most of them really just noticed one day... "Hey, I just have to smile at this guy now, and compliment her later or talk with this voice when I visit him, and then she'll give me anything I want."

People who misuse you do not like you at all, they just think you are too stupid to notice they want you to do them a favour, and they can get it every time no one else wants to help them because you are too gullible to see their only real reason for wanting to be your friend.

You just watch, stay in that friendship until you have nothing more to give... Then those people will throw you away like a squeezed-up orange. It is not healthy to stay friends with people like that, but when you try to break it, they will try to soft-talk you again. Then you need to say, enough is enough! It is over. Something important to note though, is that you probably do not believe a word you just read about certain friends here. There are things you can only learn by example, and so the best thing you can do is to see how long you will take before you become tired of that one rotten friend who uses you constantly. Good luck with that one! It is definitely hard, but somehow you will learn this lesson too if you are not strong enough to learn it by warning.

Friends are good to have, great even! We cannot live without them happy! We just have to learn how to reject the ones who does not want to respect us as much as we respect them. You can find many friends, who you could really have a great time with, then you would really be happy, and then you can really feel glad, thankful, and relaxed. You will be surprised to see how many of those good-looking, smart, and honouring people out there can become your best friends if you just go out there and talk with them.

People who can challenge you to do better, to become more and people who can really sharpen you, and be there for you too, without needing to misuse you in the process! That is why friends are there! You do not need people in your life who use you, no matter who they are.

If you are stressing about how they are feeling sometimes, do not worry, they will soon find other people who they will use and those people can motivate your lost friend. If you are out to change those friends, forget it! I am telling you now out of mountains of personal experience, it will take more than a miracle to change them, because anyone rebels when someone tries to change them.

Even you might, you just do not notice it. Just get over the friends you have lost, and get over that "attached" feeling you have to friends that misuse you, and decide to get some backbone and go out there and start talking to people and make friends who actually give as much as they get! It is time you make some friends you can benefit from too! If you do find good friends like these, do not finally come to the point where you just stress the whole time about losing them, because you only lose friends if you start to think like that.

A friend is lost before he or she is known, if we stress ourselves on how we will act with them in our presence. Once we become obsessed about what we should do by our friends, or what we would do if we lose our friends, we start to act differently. We become quiet, and we begin to over-analyse our friends to the point where we misread their gestures as personal insults toward us, while their intentions were completely innocent. We have to remember that everyone gets bad days, or bad months, and when our friends are going through a tough time, they might not be in the mood to smile as much as they once did.

It is not an insult to us, it is just a bad time our friends are going through, and it is showing through their actions, so we can be there for them. Have friends whom you can motivate, and help, and have friends that need you, and friends that you can call up just to hear about their day, and have friends that would do the same for you when you feel blue. That is why friends are there, and you can stay friends with them forever! Being alone is never fun, and if you do not go out there and greet people, you will never make friends.

Just learn to have a laugh! Did you know the greatest oak was once a little nut that held its ground?

Chapter 5.10

Problems & more tips

Did you know there ARE other things out there besides problems? Do not let your whole life only revolve around your problems! Choose to forget them sometimes, and just have a ball! Did you know everybody has some big problems out there? However, what they choose to do with them is what counts!

You can take some time to think about solutions to your problems, but give yourself a break sometimes too, and just do something you really enjoy, and think about something positive!

Have a look at these very useful tips about people:

First, let us talk about friends... It is important to know that you are a person too! Do not allow your friends to walk all over you, or to misuse you. You may be asking, "How do I do that"? Well, read on! If your friends cannot respect your decision to say no sometimes, they are not real friends, no matter what they say! Do you remember you learnt earlier in this book how to say no without anyone feeling bad? You HAVE to make some time for yourself too, or have plans of your own. If we do everything with our friends, we sometimes develop an obsession with them, without even knowing.

Also, stay away from friends who try to be the alpha-dog of the pack! Is that not just the most irritating thing if you really like your friend, but you have to stress the whole time about not saying something stupid, or not to seem your normal self? It just never works! They never care; they just always try to get something from you! You just miss a happy life because you cannot stop thinking about them, and they could not care less!

So why should you let them steal your joy? Do not allow anyone to steal your happiness! As long as they can get something, they will be happy, no matter whom it is from in the first place. Be careful for people like this! So here is that question once again: Do you think it is worth it to sit for months and think about that friend whom you lost, that so-called friend who could only call when they needed something? NO, it does not do you any good!

Do not get obsessed with people, because you are just setting yourself up to be upset! Have friends, many friends, because there are interesting people out there who could sharpen you, and motivate you, and be there for you, and you could share something with them too and do the same things for them, but do not ever let friends use you. Just always, remember to make some time for yourself too, or have plans of your own. In addition, if you ever lost a seemingly good friend, decide to get some backbone and start talking to some people out there! That friend who hurt you is not the only friend on earth! Go and have a great life full of smiles and laughs, and make many friends. Just forget about the one or two that tried to use you, so you can show them you can also get over it and be happy inside!

I would recommend that you make many friends, so many in fact that you could visit one friend this weekend, and next time you can invite someone different to visit you! Then on weekend number three, you could go see someone different again, and go out with that person for a change. You have to get busy meeting people! If you are at the movies, and you are waiting in that long queue, talk to the people in front or behind you. While you are shopping for something, and you see someone is interested in the same deodorant as you are for example, start chatting with him or her too! Really, get to know people so you can see if you would like to be friends with them, and invite them for a braai!

Actually, now that we are on the subject, there is another thing I want to ask you. Did you ever tragically lose someone you really loved a lot? You know, it is very important to go through a time of mourning about something like this. Yes, it really hurts a lot when we lose loved ones, but after that time of healing your heartache, and after you took some time to think about everything, it is time to put it in the past. No one can really tell us to be happy after losing someone dear to us. Absolutely no one had better even try! It is no one's business talking to us about our aching heart! This is something we decide to do ourselves. We want the pain to go away, but it seems like a question that has no answer sometimes.

Everyone has to face this sometime in his or her life. For most people it even happens more than once. If it had already happened to you, it must be heart shredding. The pain is unbearable. I want to tell you something about those loved ones.

Tell me something, do you really think those people are honoured and proud of you when they look down from heaven and see you wreck your life and give up on everything you care about just because they passed away? NO, they are not proud of something like that! It does not matter how they left us. Whether you had a fight and could not make up, or whether you could not say goodbye, or even if you did not have time to say, you are sorry!

Those people are in a place right now where they know everything you could not tell them, and those loved-ones understand exactly why you did those things, or why certain things happened! If you wanted to apologise for something you did, but never got the chance… Well, they know your regret! They are up there, looking at you; and they want you to have a smile on your face, and a happy heart, and they want you to have a good life!

Some of them would really like to tell you that, and I bet that if you do not start smiling and living your life to the full, you had better wear a helmet when you get to heaven! Those people you think you have lost are all going to stand there waiting to smack you over the head with a frying pan just because you gave up! Now it might be just a little hard sometimes, and you may even cry a tear or two now and then, but I will bet you can do it even with tears running down your face! It is ok to cry when you feel like it. It shows your care and love.

Is it really the end of the world? Even if we know that, we will all die someday. We will all be together again, but for now, those people we loved are up there flying, and having a good time, and waiting for the day, they can smack us over the head for giving up! They forgave you, so why torture yourself.

Let us make them happy by doing what they want us to do, and smile every day, and tell jokes, and have fun! Just know that they are living through us, inside our hearts every day, and they would smile whenever we would smile! If we are happy, they are happy! Now we can really relax, because it is all ok! They are having a good time, and we are fine, so we all win! Now go out there and have a good time so you can go to heaven one day without a helmet!

We do not even have to do the same things they used to do every day, especially if it were bad habits, because they want us to live the best life we can live and learn from our mistakes. Think about it, they are not alone, and they do not want us to be alone, so why would we ever want to stay lonely? Do you get the whole drift here? Have some fun! Go for it! You have loved ones whom are counting on you to have a happy heart!

Lastly, there is one more question for you on this topic: Do you hate yourself? Really, do you ever stand in front of the mirror and think about everything that is wrong with you? Do you ever tell yourself things like, "I am ugly", "I have a big nose", or floppy ears, or a hump back, or flat feet, or a rough skin?

Maybe you think, "my hair is not as thick", or as soft as it should be, "I talk funny", "I can't do anything right", "no one likes me", or "I'm not built as strong as any of my friends". Some people even think, "I did not experience everything my friends did"; "my skin is not as smooth and soft as those of the other girls are"; "I have an incurable disease so why worry", "I am already starting to get grey hair way before anyone else", or "I will never amount to anything"…

How about, "I will never become anything worth mentioning", "no one thinks I'm cool like they are", "I just can't ever do anything right"; "I'll never be happy", "I won't ever make enough money", or "I can't do those incredible things everyone else does"?

Well this pathetic grumbling has to stop immediately! Do you really think tearing yourself apart will solve anything? Have you ever considered looking at the 150 things that you ARE good at every day? Do you really think you will become as hot as you want to be, if you sit and think about everything that is wrong with you all day long? NO! You will not! Get out there and do something about it! Do you really think those people are who they are because they laid in bed crying and wishing for it all night long? No, they did not!

You have to remember you have a spine and, start saying: Yes I CAN! You can have a hot body! You can do everything you always wanted to do. You can be strong. You can have soft hair. You can be less sensitive to pain! You CAN do anything you set your mind to!

All you have to do is to tell yourself that you do not like being the pathetic loser you think you are, and stand up and do something about it! You have to start exercising at the gym, or even at home if you want to get a head start.

If you are thinking, "it is hard", well... It is SUPPOSED to be! How else will you become better?

Do you think a diamond becomes so beautiful because it lies there, crying for two thousand years? No, it does not! Let me tell you a little story dear reader: A diamond starts out as an enormous heap of waste. The stuff you leave in the toilet after eating too much Mexican food. When I talk big, I mean BIG, tons of the stuff. This stuff then lies there for months, simmering and fermenting in the sun.

A very huge amount of time then goes by. So much time flies, that this heap of money goes underground eventually. Yes, this actually happened right after the great rain came in the days of Noah! It lies there going nowhere and becoming nothing slowly for another endless lifetime. The pressure from the ground on top really presses down long and hard on this heap of motivation. The heat gets intense, the pressure even greater, and the disease even more so.

Yes, more time goes by, and magically, it turns into coal. The black stuff used in your braai from time to time. These coals is harder than the first stuff, so while it lies there, it needs even more time, and even more heat, yes, and even more pressure to change again. Another lifetime goes by, and magically, it changes into a rough, strong, clear, but dirty rock.

This rock lies there for another lifetime because no one noticed it, and no one knows it is there. After that time, and torture just for fun, someone stumbles upon it. It comes out of the ground, and then poof, it goes on a ring... Yeah right, not yet! These rough rocks have been hurt, and pressurised, and shovelled, and roughly handled. After these rocks come out of the ground, they go through a very harsh, high-pressure, high-heat cleaning. Then they get in the hands of a man with no mercy, and he then cuts off all the rough edges of this rock with a red-hot laser. He then forges a golden ring, and clamps this diamond on top. That is how you make a diamond. From then on, of course, this diamond is the happiest thing on earth because it is looked after carefully forever after.

If you want to become a diamond, you too are going to have to face intense pressure, heat from everywhere, endless amounts of time, and patience will be your virtue! Bang, poof, and you will be happy before you remember it!

You have to go to a therapist and get this depression chapter turned over in your life, so you can start on a new fresh blank page. Making the best and most beautiful diamonds takes a whole lot of trash, and rough edges, and a huge amount of heat, and pressure that we cannot imagine, along with time. Now stop that negative thinking and stop asking those questions! Even if you have to interrupt your mind, a billion times a day, every day! Do you want to feel better or not?

You have to shake all that negative thinking off your body and start feeling confident about what you can become! Whatever you want to do, find a way and go do it! The only one that can make something happen in your life is YOU. Yes you! I am not talking about anyone else but YOU!

If you are depressed, it can be hard to stay positive when you become positive, so every time you feel the slightest negativity you have to force yourself to read this book again so these facts can smack you over the head and get you ready to try again. Nothing is going to happen overnight, but it also does not have to take forever! You might disagree right now, and you might be determined to want to feel better in one week, but take a year and do it properly. Do it right and completely right the first time. Take the time you need to page over from depression to a clean white exciting new chapter, and do what you have to do.

You can have soft hair, and you can be an excellent fighter, you can be rich, and you can look like you want to look, and be free from addictions, and be who you want to be. You just have to go and make it happen, even if you have to try many times. Even if you have to ask for help sometimes, you can be happy again! Go to the gym, exercise. Get those adrenalin and dopamine glands to make you looking, acting, and feeling better. Get those glands to make more good chemicals so your whole body can balance its chemical-levels and make your hair softer, and your skin smoother and your mood better so you love the gym a little more. The glands in your body that creates these chemicals need to exercise.

Go to your therapist, get the anti-depressants, and get depression out of the way completely. Upgrade your diet, start moving with confidence, and try it again if you fail! One thing I can promise you is that you will most probably fail repeatedly, so you might as well jump in head over heels. You have to stop moaning, and start working without giving up at making yourself feel better about you!

Then you will be able to get everything else into your life you want to happen! Just dare to be someone who is going places! Let me show you a short poem that Marianne Williamson wrote, called "Our Deepest Fear", and it goes like this: "Our deepest fear is not that we are inadequate. Our deepest fear is that we are powerful beyond measure. It is our light, not our darkness that most frightens us. We ask ourselves, who am I to be brilliant, gorgeous, talented, and fabulous? Actually, who are you NOT to be?" You did not quite get it did you?

Let me say it again, and listen carefully now. "Our deepest fear is not that we are inadequate. Our deepest fear is that we are powerful beyond measure. It is our light, not our darkness that most frightens us. We ask ourselves, who am I to be brilliant, gorgeous, talented, and fabulous? Actually, who are you NOT to be?"

One last thing I want to tell you about relaxing is if you get a scratch on your car for example, do not freak out like a crazy person. Really, your bad feelings and anger is not going to fix the scratch. So if anything breaks, or if anything goes wrong, just try to relax.

Take a deep breath, make a plan to fix the problem, and say: "You know what, next week that problem is going to be fixed, but until then I'm not going to think about it even one more time. I am going to relax and enjoy my day, and see what new exciting things I can do because this is my life, and I'm going to enjoy it even if the world is coming to an end!"

Get the trust in you to allow other people to wash your car sometimes. If they do a bad job, do not worry about it. At least it is cleaner than it was before, and you did not have to do it. You have to think like this with everything you do, and start to like it, because that is what happy people do, and that is the only thing that will work. I promise.

This just about covers everything we had to discuss for question five, and we spoke about almost everything there is to know about depression, so now we will quickly summarize, and end off with some more motivation.

Chapter 6.1

Summary

Let me end off with a summary of what we discussed, and then I want to motivate you a little.

You can easily work everything you have learned here into a day, but it may also be overwhelming sometimes, so each week we can add one more thing to our general day. Like sleeping right, eating right, getting the right exercise, or self-motivation, all those things. Do not try to do everything at once. Just make a list for yourself, and change one habit a week, so you get used to that habit before taking on the next one. Make a plan for your every day that will eventually include everything in this book.

Now you can completely change this plan to fit your schedule, because there are people who work later, or earlier than others do. Make a plan that suits you perfectly, and remember to get your required hours of sleep, without getting any more sleep during the day, keeping busy, and not watching TV in the bedroom. Some people have adapted to sleeping with the TV or radio turned on, but it is still not healthy, and a good idea would be to adapt back to a healthy way of sleeping. It is as simple as that!

Let us have a look at one more idea of a typical day:

✓ First, we can take a nice stretch, a deep breath, and jump up out of bed at a specific time, like seven in the morning. We can get the adrenalin rushing by making our beds and brushing our teeth with a smile, having a song to whistle.

- ✓ Then we can have a nice and healthy breakfast, which is our first meal. It powers us, and rushes dopamine through our veins. Breakfast is the most important meal of the day because it 'breaks' the 'fast' of the previous night.
- ✓ Now we are ready to start the day by going to work. Keeping busy will also stimulate our bodies to make more of the feel-good chemicals we need. That is why God says: "Work is hard, but it is good for you".
- ✓ A short while after we get at work we may have a quick snack, like a favourite fruit, for more dopamine and energy.
- ✓ While we are at work, we can run to a tap and fill us with water every time we have to use the toilet. You may also drink healthy tea or juice if you took some with you.
- ✓ At lunchtime, we can eat a good portion of fresh food, and take a break from all the work-stress with a nice walk around the block with a friend, before getting back to work. Here we will not gossip. We will rather talk about an amazing thing we experienced recently, or something we plan for the weekend, for example.
- ✓ Then we can eat another snack just before it is time to leave for home.
- ✓ When we leave, we can turn on some exciting music in the car, and just listen to it without thinking about anything else. We can decide to forget about work at this time, take a deep breath, and shake your head a little while listening to your music.
- ✓ When we get home, we can kick off our shoes so we feel refreshed! Then we can make a plan to go out with some friends, or visit a family member! On other days, we can enjoy ourselves with our hobbies, like training our dog, singing, playing an instrument, swimming, reading jokes, or we can even give our cars a quick wash or do something in this time to keep us motivated and feeling great!
- ✓ Then it may come closer to dinnertime at around seven, and we may eat a healthy portion of good food while watching TV, or while chatting with someone around the dinner table. TV should not be watched for longer than one program to finish, and should not be done in the bedroom. We can spend the most of our free time with friends, and with your hobbies, using your body and keeping your biological clock turned on in the alpha state, so you can fall asleep easier later. We can then do the dishes while listening to some nice upbeat and positive

music. We might even sing along, and have a rhythm or a little dance while we tidy up. We can even go for another walk or do something active like light exercise that will keep our brain in the alpha state, so when we get ready to relax, our bodies will have a deeper fall into the sleeping beta state, allowing us to fall asleep easily.

✓ Then at around eight comes our relaxing time, where we stay far away from the bedroom, and just take some time to relax our bodies, forgetting our problems. We can take a nice soothing bath, or do some yoga or meditation on some positive thinking, we can read, or pray for someone, or we can do anything that relaxes our body and mind from stressful work or thinking fast.

✓ After we took some time to relax, at 9 we can get ready for bed by going to the toilet, drinking our last glass of water, and by making sure there are no sounds, or lights, or anything distracting in the bedroom. It has to be completely comfortable when we sleep. We can open a window to let in a cool breeze on a hot night.

✓ Then we can take a nice stretch and get into bed, lay on our back with a nice deep breath, and look at the sealing for a while. Remembering that this is the safest time for you to forget about all your problems, because there is nothing you can do about them while you are in bed, so stressing about them will only take away your sleep and give you a tired day tomorrow.

So you can just feel safe while you are in bed, and feel that great feeling of releasing your worries, and knowing that everything is ok. Tomorrow I will take on my problems, but until then everything is ok and I can stop thinking about everything. Then you can close your eyes, and sleep comfortably on your back, just thinking about sleeping every time your mind wants to wonder off. A very good idea would be to think about all the muscles in your body, relaxing one by one, starting with your toes, and ending at your eyebrows.

As you do this you can imagine you are at a perfect holiday destination you love, like the beach, or next to a river, with all your friends, and with the most perfect weather, and everything is exactly like you want it to be, and you just feel great because all your problems are magically solved. You can be there alone too, if you just need some time out of the busy usual. Soon you will drop into a deep sleep that nothing can disturb, and you will get the revitalizing rest you need to have a great time tomorrow, taking on the challenges of the day.

Now let us end-off our summary: We saw there are many types of depression, which can cause you to feel terribly down, or anxious, and with just one chemical out of balance in our bodies, it can create a whole chain-reaction of chemicals to go out of balance. Leaving our bodies tired and worn out physically, and weakened, and making us feel the pain more than others when we exercised too hard, or when we get hurt. It also causes us to hurt other people even if it was not our intention to say or do something like that.

It ultimately leaves us feeling lonely, and afraid, and sometimes worthless, and never in the mood to do anything or to go anywhere, so have we often leaved our social groups because of the fact that we really believe everything that we have told ourselves. The thing is the chemical imbalance in our bodies during depression causes us to feel bad, making us think negatively in places we did not need to think that at all. Yet we did, and we believe in those negative things even though it is not the truth.

In addition, we learnt that there are cures for almost all types of depression, and we manage others until we can find a cure. And we can do many things to keep us feeling happy, from eating better, to sleeping better, to the all-important exercise, and motivation, and spending much time with our best friends and our hobbies, and also therapy that is much more interesting and comfortable than you think, and making many more new friends.

Just remember to read this book every time you feel you are falling back into that deep hole of feeling depressed, because it will help you remember all these facts, to understand them better, and to get motivated to try again!

Before I motivate you, and end the book, I would like to tell you two interesting facts:

1. You saw that relaxing your mind and not thinking so much would make you feel a lot better. Therefore, when you exercise, or walk, or do something distracting of your problems, just use that time to forget about your problems completely and truly believe in that time that all your problems have magically disappeared. Really, you can practice it like this:

    Let us say you are going for a walk to exercise. Is there anything you can do about your problems while you are walking? No. So just, take those 5 minutes to forget about it, and believe the solution to the problem came, and everything is perfect. Believe me, it will not be the end of the world if you just decide to forget about your problems for 5 minutes.

However, you really have to forget it, far out of the back of your mind, and you have to replace it with something good like what you are going to do this afternoon, or what you plan for your weekend, or what you can do for someone who is having a hard time. If you can do this more often every day, you will find that you may be feeling a lot better, and your mind will be a lot sharper at thinking about solutions to those problems when you get back to them.

Practice imagining that you are standing on top of a mountain, dressed comfortably, and you are happy. Imagine that when you snap your fingers, all your problems fade away so you have nothing to stress about at all. Then imagine while you are on that mountain, you have an enormous power, the greatest power you can ever want. Just think that if someone tries to bother you, you can just lift up your finger, and shoot him or her with a lightning bolt, and no one can make you feel upset. That feeling you feel while thinking about this, is how you should get yourself to feel the whole time, and after exercising it often enough, you will start to notice that you can feel better without even thinking about it anymore.

2. The second fact I want to share with you is an interesting one: Did you know that you could see your normal doctor to talk to him about your depression? You can ask him to run some tests on your brain that will indicate its current state, and the results of these tests will help a psychiatrist a whole lot more at determining your type of depression, beyond doubt. This means you can get the right medication sooner, and start to feel better sooner also.

   He can also refer you to a psychiatrist he trusts. So if you feel more comfortable talking to your normal doctor, go and have a chat with him, and maybe do some tests while you're there, because the things he will tell you may just blow your mind, and finding out you're going to be ok will be even more great, and you will have the test-results to prove it.

Chapter 6.2

Motivation & a last word

So there you have it. Do whatever you have to do to be happy! You can do whatever you want to do! You have to stand up and say enough is enough! Here are some resources that can help you feel better if you struggle with depression. I included some references if you would like to know how you could help a friend of loved-one whom you think may have depression:

1. If you are a Christian, Joyce Meyer is a great motivator and teacher on the subject since she also suffered from severe depression. She is on the DSTV channel 341 twice a day, and her books and DVDs are available in shops worldwide. Battlefield of the Mind is the name of a very good teaching she created!
2. A book called, The Traveller's Gift, is a great book to read also.
3. For anxiety-related depression, Enya is a great singer of relaxing music; otherwise, you may prefer Black Eyed Peas or Shania Twain. I listen to both!
4. Try to find out even more about depression or anxiety. www.sadag.org is a great website to start with. There are many things that you might not know, and that will absolutely blow your mind! Let me show you a few examples:

   a. Did you know the seed of a peach is a cure for cancer? It breaks the protein cote around cancer cells, killing the cancer! It is bitter, but it works!

b.   Did you know Melanin is a chemical your body creates and this one decides the colour of your skin, and your hair, and even the shade of your eyes? The more melanin in your bloodstream, the darker your skin will be! It is even a natural sunscreen your body creates, meaning that people with darker skin does not get sunburn as easily as others do!

c.   Have you heard of Sodium Pentothal? Get this in your blood stream and you will struggle to tell a lie!

d.   Hey, did you know that the full moon or the alignment of the stars COULD actually influence your life, and how you feel? Think about this: The moon has a magnetic field that changes the tides at the sea. We all know that. Well, as you know, your brain uses chemicals and electronic pulses to send information around your brain. Those electronic pulses are magnetic, which means that the moon will sometimes pull harder on those pulses in your brain than other times, causing your emotions to change, and even your memory in a particular day. WOW!

e.   You can research CTS or (Carpal Tunnel Syndrome), to find ways to relax your wrists so that they are not so stiff and sore from sitting behind a desk all day! These exercises or precautions will also be good for depression.

f.   The size of your muscles and the integrity of your muscles, depend largely on the group of nerves in your body known as motor neurons.

g.   People whom are schizophrenic, cannot help they are. The cause of this problem is information leaking to places where it was not supposed to go, between the bridges of their brains, and sometimes cause them to experience hallucinations or delusions.

h.   I am telling you, you will find information that will absolutely blow your mind!

5.   If you feel that suicide is the only way out, it is not. Your life is worth living, and worth loving. There are cures for depression! You only feel hopeless because of a chemical imbalance in your body. This illness makes you want to kill yourself. If you break your arm, you would accept the pain, and apply treatment so it will feel better. The problem

with depression is that the problem is inside the reasoning of your mind, causing you to feel depressed.

How do we fight our own minds? Well, there are cures, just like there are cures for a broken arm! There is hope, you are important, and you deserve a great life. If you need to talk to someone about suicidal thoughts, or if you have a suicidal emergency, here are some free numbers you can call any time of day or night! In addition, they provide free counselling: What do you have to lose?

a. The South-African Crisis Help: 011-262-6396 (and they are available from 8am-8pm 7 days a week)
b. For an Emergency: 0800 567 567 (24 hour service)
c. Befrienders are there for e-mail help: befriend@iafrica.com
d. You may find even more numbers on the internet, for specific countries. You may even find numbers of counsellors that can help you free of charge, and you can visit them face-to-face.
e. Ronel is a therapist in South Africa that can provide therapy free of charge, and she is qualified. Her number is 082-932-4624. She will accept donations if you do not struggle with finances.
f. Here are some very helpful and important web-links to read if you would like to help someone suffering from depression:

- http://depression.about.com/cs/basicfacts/a/howtohelp.htm
- http://www.ehow.com/how_5621717_motivate-someone-depression.html
- http://www.pickthebrain.com/blog/6-motivation-tips-when-youre-depressed/ and
- http://www.socialanxietyassist.com.au/depression.shtml

Now I would like to end off the book with a personal word to you... A depressed person cannot simply "snap out of it". If a depressed person lashes out to you in anger, or say hurtful things, just remember that they are angry at their condition, not at you, and you just happen to be there.

In addition, they really need a shoulder to lean on, or an ear to listen sometimes. It is a very serious condition, and if you know someone with depression and want to help, you can! Motivating them will just be a little harder than with the usual person, and it might require that you motivate them repeatedly about the same thing, so do not give up!

It is very important to know that depression is contagious! While you help, it is very important to sometimes step back, and relax, and recharge your own batteries. Do not allow your own emotions to suffer while you are helping. How can you help someone up if both of you fell? Take a break sometimes if you start to feel it is affecting you.

Do not try to fix your loved-one's depression by yourself. It is not up to you, and nor can you. What you can do is be there for that person, and support your loved one to go for some educated therapy, and motivate that loved one to exercise and make some positive changes. Ultimately, recovery is in the hands of the depressed person, and it is not your responsibility.

You can see depression in a person if they do not care about anything anymore, or if they are just strangely sad, irritable, short-tempered, critical, moody, or suddenly quiet, or if they lose interest in everything. They also talk about feeling helpless or hopeless allot, and they seem to have a bleak or negative outlook on life, and they complain often about aches and pains. They constantly feel tired and drained, and very often withdraw from friends, family and other social activities. They sleep too little or want to sleep too much; they lose their appetite or sometimes over-eat. They very often become indecisive, forgetful, disorganised, and "out of it", and they may start using social drugs and alcohol more excessively than they should.

You may need to really educate yourself if you are helping someone cope with depression, because it is not just feelings they experience of tiredness, they really are tired physically and emotionally. Depressed people are not lazy. Try not to be offended with their actions, because it is always the depression talking. Depression makes it difficult to connect with the people they really love, on an emotional level. Just remember that hiding the problem does not make it go away. It does not help anyone involved if you cover up the problem, or lie to a friend or family member who is depressed.

If you want to help, you can try to show that person you have been feeling concerned about them lately, and that you noticed some difference in them and you are wondering how they are doing.

You can also lead by example and encourage your friend to maintain a positive outlook, to eat better, to exercise, and to lean on others for support, like happy people do to stay happy. The worst thing you can do is to expect them to look on the bright side, or to snap out of it, or that it is just in their heads, because it is not true. Even wondering why not they are better by now is a bad idea. Please read this paragraph again so you can be sure you understood this well!

You might be wondering when they began to feel like this, or what made them so depressed? Maybe you want to know how you can support them, or you might even be wondering if they thought about getting help before, or if they feel so bad sometimes that they just want to give up on trying, and it is ok to ask them about the questions you have along these lines.

It is even ok if you find a good therapist on behalf of your depressed loved-one, because it is hard for them to get in the mood of finding answers themselves, and it might be wasting their time in feeling better. Something very important to look out for is when they wish they were dead, or if they tell you, they cannot take it anymore, because this is a desperate cry for help.

Notify any therapist you can find of this immediately without thinking about anything else. If you are the depressed person, remember that it is just an illness making you feel like giving up. You are able to heal it just like a broken leg! It is not fate! If you can stand up, believing in yourself, and ask for help, you will soon feel better!

It only seems hard to ask for help, but once you get that first sentence out, you will be surprised to see how easy it really is! Do not forget that it is just an illness, and you are a very important person. Yes, you are!

It is important to listen to the depressed person, because they might not even know they have depression themselves, and to help them admit they have depression. They often feel tired, sad, guilty and misunderstood. Admitting to a loved-one that you have depression is the first step to feeling better, and it makes finding professional help and advice easier. A good idea is to get the depressed person outdoors for a few hours every day, for a short walk and a good chat in the sunlight.

This is challenging sometimes, but it is very good daily medicine. Remember, if you are the depressed person, going outside for a short while every day can really put things in perspective and make you feel comfortable as you just take in everything from the sounds outside, to the smells, and by feeling the earth underneath you. Motivate them, but do not rush them.

Depression is not fair... It is ok for us to feel like it is unfair. If you have any form of depression, it does not mean you are crazy. You are definitely not! You are ill, and you can feel better and be the exact person you really are!

If you have depression yourself, just remember that some of those around you might not understand exactly what you are going through, but they are still there for you, and want to help you! You are very important to some of those people in your life, and they love you, and care about you.

You have to fight against those low feelings, and get up even if it is the hardest thing to do in the world. Go for a walk, talk to someone about it, and find out who you can go see that will help you with a smile to overcome your depression with some anti-depressants and some talking. Do not think long-term depression will just go away on its own, oh no, it is too smart for that, so you need to get some help from soldiers with mental guns!

Stand in front of that mirror, and look at yourself. Say to yourself that you are not going to believe in those lies your brain is telling you anymore! I will do what I have to do to be strong, and to look like I have always wanted to, and if anti-depressants will make it feel less painful while I'm exercising, until my body creates enough of its own serotonin, then I will go get some, but I will live my life. Depression, you will not steal from me anymore! It is time for you to go out the door!

Remember, keep your chin up, and your chest out, and know there are many people who are behind you in your quest. Your quest to feel happy, and excited, and full of energy about your life, and they will fight with you.

The gloves are off! Go and motivate someone you know, because that will also make you feel great.

Remember that there are people you know in heaven, they are counting on you to have the best life you can have, and they will smile when you are happy because that is what they want for you. This is how you can honour them and be sure they will not smack you over the head when you get to heaven one day, for throwing your life away because of depression. Anything is possible.

If you set your mind to it, you can solve your problems, or forget about them when you are having fun, so that you are ready to take them on later. You can gym, feel great about yourself, you can look like you always dreamed of, you can be energetic, and have fun, and motivate other people so you will feel better, and you can have everything you want to have in your life. I mean everything. However, you are the only person that can make it happen! So stand up, and get busy. You do not want to reach 90 and regret that you did not do anything about your depression!

Hey, I know you can do it. I know you WILL, because you are not going to let depression win! Good Luck, you are going to do great, because you just stepped into the most awesome adventure of your life!

Before you reach the end of this book, I have one more thing to say… Listen up! You are not responsible for other people's happiness, not at all, ever, under any circumstances. This world is one vicious and horrible circle for everyone. You can either be on the stage of your own life, making sure you have fun, or you can be sitting in the audience, wishing you had the courage to stand up and do something like the other happy people. That is it. There is no middle ground. You either do it, or you do not, but it is up to you to want to learn how, and you are the one whom needs to do what you have learned! It is up to you never to give up trying, and you are the one who needs to find it in you to stand up and dust yourself off, even when no one else will help you! Choose wisely, and then go with it. One-step at a time.

Good luck out there! Now go do what you have to do!

Divine Involvement

You will be surprised if you read this! If you disagree, read it any way, just for fun!

What is hell? Most people think things like "Oh, hell... What the hell... Who cares?" Hell is actually a whole lot more scary than you think! If we can all put our worst imagination together, we still do not know what hell would be like! Did you know the Christian Bible teaches this?

Let us try to imagine a piece of hell. Now put the description from the Bible into your imagination. Your skin will boil off with the dry fire. It never dies. You will have every illness and pain known to man, at the same time. You will not see a thing, not have water to drink, and you will not be able to breathe in that brimstone smoke. Demons will break your legs, your arms, and your body. They will cut your flesh off your body while you can feel everything.

The worst things you can imagine and your worst nightmares and fears will come to life in hell. There is no escape! There will be endless screaming, gnashing of teeth, killer worms that feed on your flesh. It will never stop! Once your body is mutilated, it will return to normal, and the process starts again, forever! Imagine these things an uncountable amount of times worse. This is only the beginning!

Keep this in mind when you read this short extra piece of this book.

No one can prove the existence of the Christian God. It is not as if we can pretend to be scientists, catch God in a glass bottle, and 'observe' Him. Believing is a choice made by faith, not by observation. Do you know what an atheist is? An atheist is someone whom "does not believe", but this makes no sense! Christians cannot prove the existence of God, so they 'choose' to believe He DOES exist. Atheists cannot prove that God does NOT exist, so they 'choose' NOT to believe. Therefore, they also have to "BELIEVE" He does not exist.

Do you understand? Ok, so look at this. According to the Bible:

1. If you are a Christian and God EXISTS, you will go to heaven, so there is no problem. If you are a Christian, and God DOES NOT exist; you STILL will not have a problem, because you will then simply seize to exist after death.
2. If you are an atheist and God EXISTS, you will go straight to hell, and this is a major problem!

Does this make sense to you? Option 1 makes you double safe! Option 1 says that you will be ok if God DOES exist, AND if He does NOT exist. You make this choice on your own, completely! No one can help you with this.

Stop thinking about anything else now! Yes, you think God hurt you, but did he really? Do you tell everyone that God would not have placed us in such a terrible world? Well, God made a perfect world (Garden of Eden), and we wrecked it, by sinning! God is fixing this by creating a new world for us in heaven! Maybe we should believe in a different God? Well that is your choice. Do what your heart calls you to do, and stick with it. Just think about the possibility of going to hell. No matter what you choose, did you know there is only ONE way to get into heaven?

Yes, there is not a billion ways, just one. Let us say you never broke a single commandment in the Bible. You never ever stepped out of place in God's eyes. Did you know that you would still go straight to hell according to the Christian Bible? WHAT?! Here is proof:

1. (Romans 3:28) "Therefore, we conclude [understand] that a man is justified [going to heaven] by faith <u>without the deeds of the law</u>."
2. (Ephesians 2:8-9) "For by grace [God's love] are ye saved through faith; and that not of yourselves: it is the gift of God: Not of works [your good deeds], lest any man should boast [brag]."

What does this mean? It means you have to have 'faith' in something, to go to heaven. That is it!

Do you want to see where in the Bible God shows us the only way to get into heaven?

Ok, here it is:

1. (John 3:3-5) "Jesus answered and said unto him [Nicodemus, the friend of Jesus]: Verily, verily, I say unto thee; Except a man be born again [if he is not born again by accepting Jesus through grace as his Lord and Saviour], he cannot see the kingdom of God [he will go straight to hell]. Nicodemus saith unto him [he asked God]: How can a man be born [again] when he is old? Can he enter the second time into his mother's womb, and be born [again]? Jesus answered: Verily, verily, I say unto thee [I am telling you], Except a man be born of water [baptism] and of the Spirit [by accepting Jesus], he cannot enter into the kingdom of God [he will go straight to hell]."

To summarize, God tells us in the Bible that we can be the sweetest, most loving, kind people on earth who never sins and we will still go straight to hell, because our good deeds do not save us! If, however, we accept Jesus Christ by being born again, we will have our one-way ticket to heaven, guaranteed! God knows we will still make mistakes after we accepted Him, but luckily, God will not judge us by our deeds after we accepted Him! How great is that?

You see, because after we accepted Jesus into our lives, Jesus will be our lawyer in front of God when we die. Jesus is going to stand in front of us before God, and God will not see us, but He will see His Son, Jesus, the one who is clean! Then He will open the gates of heaven and let us go in. Amazing right? I will show you how to do this, Christian style, in just a moment.

The baptism in water is there, and it must be done right after we accepted Jesus, because it is a symbol that we went down into the grave with Jesus [we killed our sinful nature with His death], and we rose again out of the grave with Jesus [washed clean as snow, and ready to go to heaven now].

Good deeds are still important though! If you do good deeds, you are preaching about God without even using your mouth! In addition, if you do good deeds, God will build you a bigger house in heaven, and he will put more riches in your heavenly house for you! Therefore, good deeds give you a bonus! After you have accepted Jesus, and you do bad deeds, you will still go to heaven! Your life on earth will just be a complete disaster, and your bad deeds will drive God out of your spirit. So doing bad deeds long enough will cause you to lose your ticket and go to hell, but if you make mistakes after you accepted Jesus, those mistakes can be rinsed away every time with one question! "God, forgive me please? I will try my best never to do that thing again."

Go to a pastor, or read the Bible, and you will see this is true!

How can we accept Jesus Christ as our Lord and Saviour to be sure we will go to heaven one day, no matter what?

Well, one simple prayer does it (if you really mean it in your heart):

"God, I am a sinner, and I deserve to go to hell. Your Word says that You were tortured, and You died for me, so that I do not have to go through that punishment to go to heaven! I believe Your Word! Please forgive me for my sins. Wash me completely clean with your Blood, Jesus. I want to go to heaven. Jesus, I give my entire life to you. I love you, and I want You to take the wheel of my life. Please come into my life. Please live inside of my spirit as the divine trinity, forever. I accept You as my Lord and Saviour. Thank you, God! Now I am white as snow! Now the old book is thrown away, and we can begin a new blank book together! I am going to P – A – R – T – Y??? Because I am a new creature, as clean and free from sin as You are, and I will see You one day, no matter what! So I can relax because I just started over with no sin in my life! Thank you God!

Ok, but there is just one thing I am thinking about now… The devil heard my prayer too, and he knows I will not go to hell now. Jesus, I think he is going to try his best to get me back! Will You please help me Jesus, by praying for me by God? Will You please bless me with the Holy Spirit, to guide me whenever the devil comes against me? Please show me the answers! And will You please give me strong Angels out of your army, to protect me when the enemy comes against me?

Thank you, God! Now I am the happiest person on earth!

Amen."

There you have it! You have your ticket to go to heaven! Nothing and no one can take it away from you, except you! God does not judge you according to your deeds anymore!

You can only lose your ticket to heaven if you sin, and then not ask for forgiveness, and if you do not regret your sin, and try to never do those things again! This is the only way you can lose your ticket!

The point is that if you regret your sin, God knows you have learned a lesson, and you became stronger. If you do not regret your mistakes, you will not ask forgiveness and mean it, so God will not wash those things out of your spirit. This pushes God out of your spirit! Therefore, your only task after accepting Him is to try your very best for the rest of your life, to live according to God's Word.

Christians believe the Bible, the whole Bible, and nothing but the Bible, no opinions from anyone! The KJV (King James Version) of the Bible is the most accurate English translation of the Bible that exists! This is because they translated everything literally. There were many people in the KJV team, who checked these translations, to ensure that it is an exact translation from the original scriptures!

Welcome to our family of Christians!

Reference List

I would like to give special thanks and recognition to the heroes of the war in our spirits, including everyone who provided information about the topics in this book when it was researched and written. It is because of you that people can see hope again! Thank you Vincent Viljoen, Cheri Nortje, Alida Viljoen, Chris Viljoen (Senior), Margeret Brits, Caroline Brits, Wilma Smit, and everyone who helped at Marven Equipment, including those not mentioned, for your motivation and support. I love you all!

****

Printed in the United States
By Bookmasters